# The Political Economy
# of College Sports

# The Political Economy of College Sports

**Nand Hart-Nibbrig**
West Virginia University

**Clement Cottingham**
Rutgers University

**Lexington Books**
*D.C. Heath and Company/Lexington, Massachusetts/Toronto*

*Library of Congress Cataloging in Publication Data*

Hart-Nibbrig, Nand E.
  The political economy of college sports.

  Bibliography: p.
  Includes index.
  1.  College sports—Economic aspects—United States.
2.  College sports—Political aspects—United States.
3.  College sports—United States—Organization and
administration.  I. Cottingham, Clement.  II.  Title.
GV350H36     1985        338.4'7796'071173        83–48044
ISBN 0–669–06845–4 (alk. paper)

Published simultaneously in Canada
Printed in the United States of America
Casebound International Standard Book Number: 0–669–06845–4
Library of Congress Catalog Card Number: 83–48044

The paper used in this publication meets the minimum requirements of
American National Standard for Information Sciences—Permanence of
Paper for Printed Library Materials, ANSI Z39.48–1984.

The last numbers on the right below indicate the number and data of printing.

10 9 8 7 6 5 4 3 2 1

95 94 93 92 91 90 89 88 87 86

*To Robert F. Munn and Charles W. Connell*

# Contents

# Preface

One morning as I was glancing sleepily through the *Dominion Post,* Morgantown, West Virginia's daily newspaper, I was greeted with the following headline: "Rockefeller Signs Stadium Expansion Bill!" As I looked closely at the accompanying photograph, my eyes quickly focused on the happy faces so obviously enjoying the triumphant moment. Captured in this photograph was essentially what this book is all about. Here was Governor Jay Rockefeller, heir to the Rockefeller fortune and former Vista volunteer, signing the bill that would authorize expanding West Virginia University's new Mountaineer Field from a seating capacity of fifty-five thousand to sixty-five thousand, giving further evidence of the continued growth of the university's athletic program.

Seeing the governor of West Virginia signing House Bill 1851 on the shoulder of the university's head football coach was in and of itself a sight to behold. What made the picture particularly interesting was that flanking the governor and the head coach were the president of the university and the athletic director. The only persons not present to complete this symbolic picture of modern collegiate sports were representatives of the boosters and of the television industry.

In short, this study focuses on the convergence between large scale corporate interests in the form of the mass media and institutions of higher education, as well as on the links between the academic and business worlds through boosters and alumni. More specifically, this study undertakes an analysis of the economic and political forces that are changing the very character of sports generally and intercollegiate sports specifically.

Before continuing with a description of the corporate-athletic dimensions of intercollegiate sports, let me pause briefly and describe how this book began, for there is a personal story that has inspired the research and writing of this book. Like so many American boys growing up in the 1950s, I dreamed of playing football for what then was and remains today the football team of my dreams, the University of California, Los Angeles, Bruins. Like so many of my generation, I had little understanding of what big-time college sports was all about, nor did I really care. All that mattered was being able to perform in front of the many thousands who crammed the monumental Los Angeles Coliseum to watch their favorite teams do battle.

If you are wondering whether I made it to the "big leagues," the answer is no. Discounting what the lack of size and, in all honesty, perhaps the lack of exceptional ability to play with the talent being recruited at such places as UCLA, my athletic "career" was derailed during my student days at a local Catholic high school. There the realities of competitive sports were first revealed to me. The occasion of my growing up centered on my decision at age sixteen to forego any further investment of time and energy in the development of my athletic skills and to devote more time to raising a flagging grade-point average so that I could meet the high academic standards of the University of California.

While my family welcomed the decision, others did not. I was greeted with unexpected pressure not only from the coaching staff, but also from several of the priests. I will never forget the dressing down that the head football coach gave me in front of the assembled student body during a school lunch hour, when he said in clear tones that "the school did not need or want a person like me representing it." It goes without saying that it took all the strength I could muster to maintain a semblance of composure and not retreat from my decision.

Even more disappointing was the pressure that came from several priests, who similarly urged me to reconsider my decision for the sake of dear old alma mater. What in retrospect was most disturbing about this pressure was that this bandy-legged quarterback who could throw a ball with considerable accuracy was considered more important as a hunk of athletic flesh than as a growing, sensitive young man who, despite of number of obstacles, was beginning to show real academic promise. I was in Ralph Ellison's terms an "invisible man," partly because I was black and partly because my real destiny was perceived to lie in throwing a football. Needless to say, I survived all of this and entered UCLA as a freshman in the mid-fifties.

During my undergraduate years at UCLA, I saw up close what so many have come to expect from a system of athletics which cares mostly for athletic production and virtually nothing for the academic and intellectual development of the many young men who put on football cleats or basketball sneakers to carry the banner of colleges and universities across the country.

It was at UCLA that I began to understand more fully the depth of the business of college sports. There was just too many of my old "running buddies" who would not have been on campus if it had not been for their exceptional athletic talents. I remember tutoring one of them, a star defensive end on the football team who needed a "D" in order to maintain his eligibility. My friend got his "D," kept his eligibility, had a short fling in the pros, and ran into trouble with the law after his football career ended. I don't believe he ever graduated. Little did any of us realize that my friend would be just one in a long and continuous line of what Harry Edwards has called black "paid gladiators," whose only function was to provide entertainment for those on and off campus.

With the sixties came the heightened interests and sensitivities of the black community which for a brief moment extended to athletics and found their pitoval moment in the black power salute at the 1968 Olympics in Mexico City. I can still recall the adverse reaction to this gesture in the national press and among those responsible for the ideological purity of "amateur" sports. I remember as well how many of us in the black community reacted to the courage and symbol of black resistance to racial oppression and our growing optimism about being able to do something about that oppression. We would mobilize where our numbers were the strongest, and athletics, it seemed then, was one area in which the black presence could be translated into black power.

We were wrong. We simply could not anticipate the many forces that would come together and change fundamentally the thrust of the black power movement and reduce its effectiveness. Also, we did not anticipate the power of the American business system and the growth of the power of mass media, especially television, to transform the system of sports production in the United States. The growing commercial and corporate-athletic dimension of college sports is the most important fact in this study. It has been this development from amateurism to corporate athleticism that has swept aside or absorbed all other competing values traditionally associated with athleticism in institutions of higher education. Likewise, under the rubric of corporate athleticism Harry Edward's notion of paid gladiators takes on even greater significance. This book attempts to analyze this sports business system that we call corporate athleticism.

*Nand Hart-Nibbrig*

This study is certainly not a history of college sports, nor is it a history of the American university. Rather, it is a tentative and obviously incomplete interpretation of the dual transformation of college sports and the American university. The sources of this transformation revolve around the overthrow of amateurism as a guiding ethos for the organization of college sports in American universities. More specifically, the study endeavors to trace in general terms the evolution of corporate athleticism in American universities, the newly emerging relationship of athletics to market forces external to the university and to the determinants of that evolution. This study should therefore provide insight into how markets emerge in previously traditional, nonmarket institutions to infuse new commercial meaning into organized activity in American society.

My interest in this topic grows out of my study of Thomas Kuhn's paradigms in scientific revolutions. As is the case with amateurism, old concepts persist as descriptions of reality long after they themselves cease to accord with reality. Amateurism is no longer an adequate descriptive term for certain sports played at American universities. I have been particularly struck, however, on many occasions by the public's apparent disenchantment with the monetary aspects of college sports and of sports generally. By and large, the American public draws back from the more crass features of sports commercialism, whether professional or amateur. This resistance was one of the first clues that something about college sports had changed fundamentally. At the same time, few observers have sought to formulate a definition of such changes; or, at least, to view the changing character of sports as indicative of important changes in American society. Nor have many observers seriously tried to conceptualize what many commentators mean by big-time athletics. This study seeks to do so, by examining the power of economic and political forces on the organization of college sports.

As I perceive it, the most significant change in college sports is that they now function as a new system with strong links to social and political forces external to the university. As is suggested in the final chapter, universities on the make use sports to position themselves politically, above all to capture political attention, and to garner new financial resources as part of an institutional expansion strategy. In many instances, going big-time in college sports can play a part in improving a university's national academic rank.

In short, changes in the role of college sports are sometimes politically induced and can often be traced to positioning strategies. At one level, we argue that amateurism was overthrown at public universities because its political reach was severely limited. Amateurism could thrive at a time when universities were strongly oriented toward their internal mission, but the rise of corporate athleticism indicates the external emphasis of the university, its more sensitive orientation toward its external constituencies. In the 1980s, the role of public universities as producers of high technology in scientific research and of mass entertainment in sports has strengthened their dependence on public resources. In this context, universities behave much like nations using sports to celebrate their glory and to advance their foreign or external policies at the expense of domestic sectors.

*Clement Cottingham*

# Acknowledgments

There are many people we want to thank for their assistance in writing this book. Some helped us indirectly by influencing our thinking, others helped us directly as we approached the task of preparing the manuscript. In the first category we would like to acknowledge a great debt to David Nelson, Norman Auburn, Benjamin Tuchi, Harold Hart-Nibbrig, Joel Rogers, Robert Munn, and Charles Connell. Without their timely and incisive comments and criticisms our task would have been more difficult.

We also acknowledge the debt all of us owe to Harry Edwards, whose work on behalf of exploited athletes continues to be a beacon of insight and reason in this age of commercial exploitation.

Thanks to Suzanne Summers Tok, Elizabeth Pool, Debbie Koon, Martha Johnson, and Sharon Fox for their assistance and patience with our endless redrafting of the text. We have once again learned how important good editors are to the enterprise of writing. We owe our gratitude and respect to John Luchok and Dorothey Sedley at West Virginia University, and Martha Cleary at Lexington Books. They made sure that our drafts and final copy had a professional touch and that many of our dangling abstractions were eliminated.

Special thanks to David Williams, who in a time of fiscal stringency found the necessary support without which this manuscript could not have been completed.

Lastly, we want to thank the many people who listened to our ideas and who encouraged their publication. They are the real audience for this book.

*Nand Hart-Nibbrig*
*Clement Cottingham*

# The Political Economy
# of College Sports

# 1
# Introduction

This book traces the evolution of college sports, with particular attention to the political and economic factors that directly and indirectly shape the structure of collegiate sports, and to the systemic problems associated with that evolution. This systems approach underlines the problems developing from weak institutional controls in the governance of college sports. For example, universities and the National College Athletic Association (NCAA) have failed by and large to contain the commercial aspects of sports. Indeed, the NCAA in particular has done much to define the new sports system. Despite their professed concern with maintaining academic values, university presidents have yet to design new procedures for containing the commercial aspects of sports on the campus, and they are not likely to do so.

We use the term *corporate athleticism* to refer to the influence of the business ethic on the new sports system. Above all, this ethic emphasizes being "number one," securing large gate receipts and numerous, lucrative television appearances, on hiring the right coaches and recruiting the "blue-chip" athletes to ensure those incomes. The ability of college sports programs to muster resources for advanced training infrastructures, to adopt high performance standards, and to recruit and train athletic talent is the functional outcome. The concept of corporate athleticism is useful in that it facilitates the more rigorously systemic interpretation of college sports offered here. It concentrates on resolving persistent anomalies that other writers have also noted, and strives for what we hope is a deeper, more encompassing interpretation of the basic structure of college sports. In effect, the term bestows new meaning on the popular saying that college sports are simply big business.

The notion of amateurism was central to college sports before the second World War. Although the term connotes many things, it refers mostly to sports played purely for fun. The social ethos of amateurism's genteel tradition did not require financial remuneration for sports activity, so that in this sense, amateurism was in fact a class ethos in which the college athlete, like his class counterparts outside the university, was not compelled to engage in commercial activity. Over time, however, this ethos spread to the general population, which still idealizes the athlete in amateur terms, as someone whose behavior is not dictated solely by commercial values. Although many Americans still embrace a romantic conception of amateurism, the notion of sports activity as an end in itself has long since dissipated. To be sure, sports are still associated with fair play, self-development, and other worthy virtues, but this amateur ideal exists mainly in symbolic terms.

At the college level, the amateur concept has steadily eroded in the face of relentless commercialization. College sports are increasingly associated with money; the salary of coaches, the commercial aspirations of the stellar athletes, and the emphasis on television contracts all highlight the fact that key actors in the college sports system are motivated by economic considerations. College sports have become increasingly money-minded—one of its recent and dominant characteristics. The reality of modern sports involves a great deal of money: informal remunerations in the form of athletic scholarships; underground payments to newly recruited college athletes; or indirect payments, like those provided to Olympic athletes in order to preserve their increasingly fictive amateur status. With the growth of commercialization, the athlete no longer engages in sports for himself and for self-development. In the evolving commercial conception of sports, the emphasis in the college sports system is primarily on output, requiring not surprisingly, the creation of a winning team. As the commercialization of college sports advances, athletes spend more time training to be professionals, so that in this important respect, college sports come more and more to resemble professional sports.

The increased commercialization in college sports has given rise to a new sports system, that we call *corporate athleticism*. The behavior of athletes in this system can be better understood in terms of behavioral standards associated with corporate athleticism, not with amateurism. Though amateurism continues to shape our image of sports—a notion inherited from early conventions of sports behavior—the behavior of contemporary college athletes rests on behavioral premises quite different from those associated with the older amateur tradition of college athletics. Truly, the amateur sports system has been overthrown and replaced by a far more complicated sports system, one that we shall define in the following chapters. In the new sports system, commercialism is the driving force, offering powerful, tangible rewards to winners in college sports. College sports are now closely tied to the market system, they are an extension of and reflection of modern, late twentieth-century American capitalism. Although we frequently refer in casual conversation to college sports as big-time business, few of us have devoted much thought to how big and in what sense college sports is really a business.

In what follows, we trace the rise of corporate athleticism in terms of certain important indicators. For one thing, college sports are corporately organized, in the sense that their dominant personality derives from their operating like a business and that the nature of their profit is winning. Our analysis concentrates on football and basketball because they are the two most highly developed corporate sports. Not all college sports, however, are organized on a corporate basis. Other college sports may contain some elements of corporate sports, but they remain predominantly amateur because winning in these sports does not produce a profit or substantial publicity for the university. Most public universities now include a highly commercialized sports sector and a largely noncommercialized amateur sector. Not all public universities have developed corporate athletics, for it is becoming increasingly difficult to organize or sustain corporate athleticism; it is a serious business and not every public university can do it. Finally, we should note that many private universities and colleges—for reasons we discuss later—are relatively strong bastions of amateurism. Yet even they are infected with the virus of corporate athleticism; even at the Ivy League universities coaches can be fired for sustaining a losing tradition. Thus, we claim that amateurism in its pure form no longer exists at the college level.

College sports have become more corporate over the past three decades. These sports have become more separate from the university, just as the modern corporation is now characterized by the separation of management from ownership. Many coaches are paid corporate salaries amounting to hundreds of thousands of dollars. The students in college athletic programs have also been affected by these changes. Though affected by recent reforms, student-athletes have in many ways become increasingly separated from the student body (indeed, the adoption of the "student-athlete" designation disguises this separation). In fact, corporate athleticism brings about the separation of student and athlete. Some student-athletes from lower-class families are not in college to get an education. In the 1960s and 1970s, the student-athlete tended to devote less than priority attention to his college grades. Many studies now assert, surprisingly, that athletes perform as well academically as other college students.* For the most part, however, many athletes are not in college to attain passing grades, though many eventually do graduate. Increasingly, athletes receive informal remuneration; promises of gifts, cars, lump-sum payments, and no-show jobs are now apparently standard features of the college recruitment process. These payments by enthusiastic alumni boosters impart the lesson to athletes that college sports pay. Above all, the talented athlete is taught that he is on campus primarily to enhance his skill acquisition in sports.

College sports are also corporate in an institutional sense. As sports have become more commercialized, the sports sector within the university has grown institutionally. The management structure of college sports have

---

*Conversation with Eric Zemper, Research Director for the NCAA. Prior to release of studies on academic performance by student participation in Div. 1 sports.

become less personal and more bureaucratized. A hierarchy of coaches follows specific training procedures in the organization of standard sports routines. The practices, the movement of students through the sports hierarchy, the review of plays, and the scouting of opposing teams all make college sports quite parallel to professional sports. In addition, the existence of the sports dormitory, the modern training facilities, and the appearance of the ever-larger sports stadia (with usually between fifty thousand and eighty thousand seats) all form part of the architectural structure of corporate athleticism. The corporate infrastructure grows ever larger as market forces penetrate the university, as the relationship between college sports and mass entertainment grows stronger. This bundle of indicators reveals the intimate links between college sports and contemporary markets. Qualitatively, these changes have brought about the intercollegiate athletics system we term corporate athleticism.

Another important component of the new sports system is athleticism. Whereas the term *corporate athleticism* indicates broad, institutional change in the way college sports are organized and rewarded, *athleticism* in this context refers to sports behavior, characterized particularly by the pervasive emphasis on winning at all costs. In the new sports system, ever greater rewards go to winners. This fact shapes the intensity with which high school and college athletes participate in sports. Although athleticism clusters mostly in highly competitive sports and in the more fully developed sports programs, it is not, strictly speaking, confined exclusively to highly commercial sports. Rather, athleticism as a behavioral standard is associated in all college sports with heightened competitive intensity. One study, for example, noted among male students in public and parochial schools, grades three through twelve, "the diminishing importance of the fairness factor [playing the game fairly] and the increasing importance of the success factor [that is, beating one's opponent] as age increases."[1] It is, above all, this increasing emphasis on winning that characterizes the attitudes and behavior of contemporary athleticism. As young people age and become more deeply involved in organized high school and college sports, they evidently become more committed to athleticism.[2]

This new athleticism involves long-term, laborious training. Greater athleticism in college sports produces more intensive and more extensive training. Indeed, more and more the development of prime athletes depends on access to advanced training techniques and machines, and accordingly, the normal "play" associated with amateur sports is transformed into work. In a study of eleven-year-old, middle-class boys, it was reported that "participants in organized sport considered skill or victory as the most important factor in play while nonparticipants stressed the factor of fairness."[3] Such attitudes, according to several authors, help socialize young people into highly competitive roles.

Central to the commercialization process of college sports is the all-consuming aspect of the activity. Whenever commercialization appears, it displaces an existing political or institutional interest. With respect to the student-athlete, critics contend that the player's interest as a student in securing an education is displaced by the material interest of succeeding as a professional athlete. Since the payoffs for success in sports are so great—professional sports being a last, powerful stronghold of Horatio Algerism—the athletic interests of individual sportsmen frequently displace academic values, like individual study and learning as ends in themselves. As a result of this displacement, many so-called student-athletes end up attaining neither a college education nor the status of *outstanding* athlete that is required to gain access to professional sports.

When athletes complete four or five years of college without receiving an education, people often conclude that universities have exploited them. Many athletes toil long and hard in the college locker rooms for four or five years, but few can claim to have been educated in return for hard work on college fields or courts. Notwithstanding, college officials frequently argue that on average athletes do as well educationally as nonathletes. According to a recent survey by NBC of athletes at Division I schools, 30.5 percent of college athletes graduate in four years; 39.4 percent graduate in four and a half years; and 55.5 percent graduate in five years. These graduation rates are not strikingly dissimilar, these sports officials contend, from those of nonathletes.

Another indicator of the increased competition in college football is the practice of redshirting. Begun in the 1950s, this practice involves having students not participate in organized sports during their freshman year, thus enabling athletes to remain in college for five years. Redshirting enhances a school's competitive position and extends the athletes' sports apprenticeship. According to an NBC poll, 95 percent of all Division I schools redshirt. At Nebraska, for example, 81 percent of all football players are redshirted. In the view of the University of Nebraska's athletic director, the practice provides athletes with five years of scholarship and gives them a better chance of graduating. However, redshirting also constitutes part of athleticism since it extends a student's *athletic* career an extra year. Whatever the benefits, redshirting adds at least one year to the college career of many athletes. And, needless to say, this practice stabilizes the dominant position of those teams at the very top of the football and basketball hierarchy.

This chapter has mentioned some of the results of corporate athleticism. In the next chapter we will examine some of the moving forces behind this new sports system to see how they relate to the American university.

# Notes

1. John Loy, in J. Alex Murray, ed., *Sports or Athletics: A North American Dilemma* (Windsor, Ontario: University of Windsor, Canadian-American Seminar, Press 1974), 91.

2. Maloney and Petrie (1972) cited in Loy, in *Sports or Athletics,* 91.
3. Loy, in *Sports or Athletics,* 92.
4. Presented on television, 1 December 1984.

# 2
# Corporate Athleticism:
# A New Sports System

On June 27, 1984, the U.S. Supreme Court decided, in a major anti-trust suit brought by the Universities of Oklahoma and Georgia, that the National Collegiate Athletic Association (NCAA) could no longer act as the sole distributor of college football games to national television networks. In effect, this decision made each college or university a seller in a newly deregulated sports television market and instigated a helter-skelter scramble to gain access to the largest prime-time sports audiences. It is far too early to say with any certainty exactly what will emerge when the dust finally settles. It is not too early, however, to offer a few thoughts on the emergence of what appears to be a new sports system in the United States, a system whose structures are becoming increasingly clear with every passing season.

We have chosen to call this system corporate athleticism. The term as we use it here refers to the influence of the business ethic on the new sports system. Above all, it connotes the introduction of commercial values as the basic organizing principle of competitive college sports.

As was pointed out in chapter 1, corporate athleticism places winning above all else, as the number one priority. It expends great effort (investment) to recruit, train, and develop top athletes (workers) and to find and reward "winning" coaches (management). Winning football or basketball (the product) will then generate, if all goes well, substantial gate receipts and numerous television contracts (profit). The separation of the stadium from the campus at many universities, the appearance of the student athlete before massive national television audiences, and the systematizing of national recruiting efforts at prominent public universities all constitute key ingredients of corporate athleticism.

With the emergence of corporate athleticism at U.S. colleges and universities sometime in the early 1960s, the scale of college sports has undergone a remarkable transformation, whose full momentum is only now being recognized. By its very nature, the new sports system is bound to grow into a more fully integrated competitive system of commercial college athletics. Calling this system *corporate athletics*—gives us an opportunity to analyze it as a system, to concentrate on the persistent anomalies of college sports as *business* that other writers have noted, and to strive for a deeper, more encompassing interpretation of the basic structure of college sports.

The integration of mental and physical education in public universities has consistently posed problems for American higher education, and many have discussed the role of sport and its contribution to the intellectual and personal development of college students. At present, there are a number of issues centering on the various ways that sports training compromises academic values within the university: whether the existence of a commercial sports program undermines the academic integrity of universities; the extent to which higher education itself makes the emergence of corporate athleticism inevitable by providing special support for an increasingly commercial activity which seems less and less related to the inherent aims of higher education; and finally, whether universities can effectively regulate the new sports system within the scope of academic rules and administrative requirements.

The university's support for college sports is evident in the financial resources provided athletic programs, the relaxation of academic standards for student athletes, and the substantial functional autonomy bestowed upon athletic departments' coaches and directors. The largest athletic departments within the ranks of football and basketball powers resemble business corporations more than they do older athletic departments; they have considerable functional autonomy from other aspects of the university organization. In spite of the recent efforts of college presidents, meeting at the NCAA in 1983, to develop new controls over athletic programs, the containment of athleticism is likely to prove only temporary at best, for the commercialization of college sports is not a recent trend. On the contrary, the realities of sports commercialism have influenced intercollegiate athletics almost from the beginning.

## Historical Continuity

Seen in these terms, a most distinctive feature of the commercialization of college sports is its historical continuity. In fact, a careful reading of the historical literature indicates the early presence of commercialism in college sports. In this formative period, sports were not well organized and existed in many respects without the standard institutional structures and procedures now associated with modern intercollegiate athletics. Yet college sports, especially football, did reflect the aggressive commercialism of the latter part of the nineteenth century. Football grew rapidly in popularity, and the entrepreneurial spirit associated with the development of the modern business corporation became part of the university sports atmosphere.

In retrospect, one is struck by how quickly the university accepted corporate norms and values. The entrepreneurial social process was accepted as given, and, in turn, university presidents of the period used the pervasive influence of the business corporation to generate social, political, and financial support for the university. Thus began a process and a relationship which endures, albeit in different form, even today. In the first quarter of the twentieth century, one commentor argued that the president and faculty should defend the university against the onslaught of sports commercialism. But casual observation suggests that faculty participation in university governance declined during the 1970s and 1980s.

The university's confederal organizational structure also facilitates the emergence of corporate athleticism by granting its subunits substantial administrative autonomy to carry out their specialized educational missions. Though many academic units enter into client relationships of various sorts with outside groups, the athletic departments have become sports production systems and have actively formed client relationships with boosters and with local business interests. In view of the weak presidency in the university, the fragmented governance structure of the decentralized public university does not permit beleaguered presidents to control actively or closely monitor relationships between the athletic complex and external political interests.

Not surprisingly, the pressures toward corporate athleticism dominate. The university can adapt to the pressures of market forces and to political interests associated with college athletics, but it cannot easily control them. Television, as a dominant component and the principal market mechanism of the sports production system, now structures all other institutions, including universities and their athletic programs. Because the athletic complex's relation to the market mechanism and to the highly organized set of clientele interests is so well developed, the university's adaptation processes are almost predefined. Political fiefdoms within the university merely reinforce the adaptation process, giving the athletic complex a degree of political autonomy that far exceeds that available to the traditional academic units in the university. Moreover, the currently shrinking resource base of the university, reinforces pressures for the university to forge new relationships with commercial, industrial, government and other external sources of financial support.

The university athletic complex is directly linked to expanding market forces (that is, to television and to mass-appeal sports) and is at the same time more removed than other administrative units from the academic values that permeate other sectors of the university. Individuals recruited into the corporate athletic complex are recruited not as students, but primarily as potentially successful players of quasi-professional intercollegiate athletic roles. In various ways, for example, through the distortion of academic recruitment criteria, the low graduation rates for prominent athletes, or the inflated grades given athletes—the university validates the athletes' extra-academic status. In effect, the university's accommodation to the sports market is pervasive and self-perpetuating. The trend toward corporate athleticism is reinforced and, often, encouraged by the traditional processes of higher education.

On the historical evidence, the commercialization of college sports is not inherently incompatible with the maintenance of academic values. As sports commercialism in the universities has steadily expanded, overall academic standards at universities have in fact risen. Even as criticism has grown, universities have further legitimized sports commercialism by organizing special remedial activities to improve the low academic performance of numerous athletes. This is an adaptive measure, however, and it, along with the historical record, merely illustrates the extent to which the athletic complex at schools with major sports programs remains functionally separate from the university. Though public criticism of sports commercialism persists, the continued development of the new college sports system seems to be irreversible.

## Consequences of Corporate Athleticism

Structural tensions exist at many points in this evolving sports system; nevertheless, it seems clear that expansionary competitive impulses are an important component of corporate athleticism. Assuming that this assertion is valid, it is important to determine how each institution works to sustain or accommodate the interests of corporate athleticism and to examine existing trends in corporate athleticism.

### The End of Amateurism in Intercollegiate Athletics

More than ever, it seems clear that the reign of the amateur in intercollegiate athletics has ended. The present system of intercollegiate sports is highly professionalized. Whereas the amateur participated in intercollegiate athletics as a division from mental activity, the corporate athlete performs as a diversion for others. He (or she) performs before a mass audience with high expectations of reward and recognition. Clearly, the character of the contemporary sports regime, with its emphasis on specialization and pecuniary gain, indicates that the new sports system rests on values fundamentally different from those associated with the high culture of amateurism.

Strictly speaking, an amateur in sports may be considered one who participates in his leisure without extensive training, and without financial, social or other significance attached to winning or losing; the corporate athlete, on the other hand, participates in sports full time, requiring intensive and extensive training, ultimately to secure financial remuneration and all the prerequisites of a professional career. As has been pointed out before, corporate athleticism is characterized above all by competitive intensity and by an emphasis on winning at any cost.

### Increased External Influence (Especially Market Forces) on Intercollegiate Sports

The most important external influence on college sports is television. Television plays and will continue to play the primary role as a structuring mechanism of corporate athleticism. It performs this pivotal role primarily by creating, promoting, and organizing highly lucrative sports markets. Television occupies this niche in corporate athleticism because it has the ability to organize mass appeal for its products.

Through such means, television stimulates competition between universities interested in gaining maximum access to scarce television time. Rather than simply compete against one another, the superstar university athletic teams compete for attendance, national or regional television time, and revenue. These benefits to a university are influenced substantially by a team's ability to obtain access to nationally televised markets. Television creates both the collegiate superstar and the superpowers. Access to the lucrative sports system associated with performance on television defines the corporate nature of the new sports system, and television supplants the universities and colleges as the prime producer of sports. The fact that nearly all college sports teams strive to penetrate national television markets defines the boundaries of corporate athleticism. Those universities that do not penetrate television markets will perforce remain amateurs.

Finding so-called amateurs in the college ranks these days is becoming increasingly difficult. With the expansion of cable television systems, universities that would otherwise have been locked out of television have found new opportunities for exposure and revenue. Even the Ivy League has been moved to seek sport respectability through regional telecasting of their games.

Television dramatically raises the financial stakes associated with college sports. Since the sports market is finite, television contracts are offered to those teams that can most easily attract a large television audience because they are consistent winners. In this way television can easily generate extensive markets, and the increasing diversity of sports events on television indicates the growing potential of this market. Indeed, the overall success of college sports in attracting television audiences has increased the range of the sports market to include tennis, golf, hockey, and soccer, as producers seek to attract additional television audiences. But competition between universities and among sports increases the segmentation in the sports market—a trend likely to persist in the 1980s.

The universities' newly won right to negotiate directly with television networks for appearances will extend the scope of corporate athleticism. For one thing, universities will deepen their orientation toward the commercial system. Athletic departments will be free to bargain with television networks on the basis of their individual market positions. They will, accordingly, possess greater incentives to establish and maintain a clearly defined market position. Universities, therefore, seem likely to adapt even more to television markets as a result of having won the right to negotiate directly for appearances with national or regional television networks.

Consequently, the role of market forces in intercollegiate sports will grow larger as more universities henceforth compete directly for market position as determined by successful television appearances. At the same time, however, the deregulation of college sports will place universities in a more dependent position vis-a-vis television producers. Such producers, in turn, will become more powerful in that they can select sports contests on the basis of audience appeal and on the resulting willingness of advertisers to pay more to sponsor such appearances.

But there is a cloud over this scenario. For some major college programs expecting financial gain from television, disappointment looms. As more games are televised, the television audience is also becoming more fractured, and this means, among other things, that there will be fewer advertising dollars and thus fewer dollars for America's prime athletic powers. In the meantime, the hunt for revenue for these expensive programs continues unabated.

In sum, the American university's accommodation to the new television market forces is considerable. The universities are more deeply enmeshed in a rapidly evolving sports market than many realize, and the competition among universities for access to this expanding sports market is growing. Although the university's external relations in other commercial areas may, perhaps, be congruent with the maintenance of academic values, in the area of sports, the sports market dominates in its relationship with the university. For example, the requirements of television structure the sports market for a given university, and accordingly the university builds a new stadium to accommodate its large-scale markets. Universities also alter their sports schedules to respond to television presentations. In these and in other ways, universities, undertake actions that increase the ability of market forces to determine intercollegiate athletics.

### Boosters and Corporate Athleticism

A distinctive feature of successful college sports teams is that they all have strong booster groups. As corporate athleticism grows, boosters are likely to become more important, for they generate competitive intensity, encourage gifts, and provide strong support for intercollegiate sports. While these functions are not confined to contemporary boosters, they create seemingly indispensable conditions for the penetration of television markets. This situation poses some important questions. What is it about boosters that makes them indispensable to the new sports market system? How does the expansion of television markets influence their evolving role? And finally, what actions of boosters help intercollegiate teams move from the amateur level to the corporate athletic system?

Boosters influence the system in several ways. First of all, they provide an informal system of fringe benefits: local radio and television programs for coaches, assistance with transportation costs, educational benefits for coaches' children, investments in stocks and real property, special banking and mortgage arrangements, and sundry other benefits. Boosters also contribute to the productivity of the sports system through their roles as managers of an underground economy that raises a substantial amount of money to provide surreptitious benefits like cars, women, money, organization, and other remunerations to athletes and coaches. In this way the boosters build a financial and economic infrastructure, providing the foundation for serious intercollegiate competition. Without a strong booster support system, universities are unable to compete in the new commercial sports system. As universities become more closely integrated into this system, they also become more dependent on boosters. Hence, boosters are likely to become more active in the emerging corporate athletic system because of their ability to respond quickly to changing market impulses.

Another way in which boosters influence the system is by building vertical linkages to similar groups at junior colleges and at the high schools. This deepens the capacity of the university sports systems for incorporating other aspects of the secondary and higher educational system. For example, as the boosters become active in the secondary schools and in the community, they influence parents to become booster agents for their children, and these parents provide the resources to enhance the competitive spirit of their children.

In these ways the culture of corporate athleticism penetrated deeply into American society and into culture at large, and boosters are the most pervasive agents of that penetration. They function as an informal mechanism for extending the scope of the new sports system, and through this and other mechanisms, games have assumed a new importance in shaping the broad competitive impulses in American society.

*　　*　　*

A highly decentralized sports system of massive scope is now evolving in the United States. It is a total sports system, characterized by top-to-bottom integration of the corporate television system and intermediary social structures. The sports television market induces all intermediary structures—universities, boosters, and highly competitive families—to serve market ends.

This penetration capacity mobilizes individual talents on a massive scale around the norms of the sports market. All the intermediary institutions adjust in varying degrees to the market impulses of corporate athleticism. *The distinctive essence of the new athleticism is that business values are now deeply embedded into a new production system with a substantial capacity to penetrate the larger society.* This penetration has a corrosive effect in that it filters out values—including the values of amateurism and fair play—that seem to be incompatible with the business ethos of corporate athleticism.

## The NCAA and the Legitimation Crisis

In periods of flux, the NCAA has sought to restructure athletic participation through new regulatory procedures. Formulating new rules is one way in which the NCAA has tried to adapt to changes in the fundamental structure of sports; this response to change is particularly important for the NCAA since its organizational structure developed in the context of amateur athletics, and in amateur athletics, the universities were the primary sponsors of intercollegiate sports. But the NCAA is a weak institution operating on cooperative norms to punish violations by universities of amateur athletic rules. In the era of corporate athleticism, however, the prime sponsor of intercollegiate sports is television, and by and large, the NCAA has not been very effective in establishing a balance of power between the television networks and the universities. The recent Supreme Court decision diminishing the already declining power of the NCAA has all but destroyed the association's regulatory role and constitutes another important constraint on the NCAA's ability to deal with the expansion of television's power over sports markets.

This reduction in the NCAA's ability to regulate intercollegiate sports appears likely to continue in the future. Naturally, the NCAA has resisted measures that would diminish its regulatory authority, but without much success. Universities with strong athletic traditions have gained a much sought-after autonomy that they are unwilling to relinquish; they also possess the resources to adapt well to new, expanding television markets. In addition to being challenged by the universities most responsive to television markets, the NCAA has lost authority as a result of the increased pluralism in universities generally, pluralism in the sense that internal power in universities has become more fragmented. For example, the limited power of university presidents over sports programs has brought about cross-cutting political pressures within the NCAA. In one case, when the American Council on Education sought to organize a reform council, the resulting coalition of university presidents was not supported in important instances by coaches and athletic directors. This kind of political fragmentation among university representatives makes it especially difficult for the NCAA to organize a wide-ranging policy consensus. Finally, the NCAA has found it most difficult to regulate the activities of boosters, who of course have no formal status in the new sports system.

The regulatory role of the NCAA remains uncertain in a sports system in which the emphasis on market values seems clearly destined to become stronger. The amateur origins of college sports provide the rule-making foundations for the NCAA's role, and yet the amateur values of college sports have experienced a profound decline for many decades. At the same time, the NCAA itself is not structured to function as a strong regulatory body. Recent events have shown once again that its authority is not strong enough to contain the powerful market thrust of corporate athleticism. The organizational structure of college sports in its new corporate form is at the same time inside and outside the university and thus by its very nature is subject to a set of social and business norms very different from those amateur norms historically connected to college sports and higher education.

## Conclusion

The more corporate major college athletics become, the more they move away from the amateur concept as the model for all sports participation. The inner content of competitive college sports now depends on organization, selection, and training, and the ethics of the new sports order solidly embraces the notion of winning as the number one priority. In large areas of American life, the individual becomes a significant actor only when as new talent he is harnessed to a specialized organization, and the world of college sports is no different. Although individual effort in sports retains an honored place as the indispensible basis for teamwork, the scale of the modern sports organization in important respects simply dwarfs the individual. The amateur athlete represents raw talent; the corporate athlete in modern college sports represents trained talent—the product of intensive and highly articulated sports training.

Television will continue to structure corporate athleticism by creating new requirements to which universities, players and teams will adapt. Athletic directors will redouble their efforts to find the resources needed to strengthen the new athletic structure. In some instances, universities may even use their political clout to gain access to regional television markets, and the universities' accommodation to corporate athleticism will increase.

The rise of television marked the end of amateurism in college sports. Amateurism was not linked to corporate values or beholden to mass audiences, and as a result the values of athleticism did not come into play. Under the influence of television, however, corporate athleticism increasingly operates as a relatively pure market system, recruiting and training students for careers in professional sports. Moreover, it reduces the university's ability to promote athletic values that possess no inherent exchange value in the market place, that is, those values associated with noncommercial sports.

The rise of corporate athleticism brings about value displacement, as the value attached by society to the individualism of the inner-directed, disciplined, amateur sportsman dissipates. Athletes are now nurtured on the values of corporate teamwork and competition for positional goods, that is, media exposure and product expansion. At the same time, corporate athleticism glorifies the individual of exceptional talent, the superstar, yet as the 1984 Los Angeles Olympics often revealed, superstars do not always represent the triumph of inner values.

To summarize, that television changes the scale of the major college programs makes clear its corporate contribution. Few observers associate amateurism in college sports with mass audiences, for amateurism neither represents modern corporate values nor requires mass audiences for its presentation. Under the influence of television, however, major college sports programs operate increasingly as relatively pure, large-scale market systems, which recruit and train student-athletes to be professional athletes. Further, the rise of corporate athleticism brings in its wake value changes, as the individualism of the inner-directed, disciplined amateur is displaced. Even athletes playing for fun frequently aspire to a certain ruthless perfection associated with more "elevated" corporate athletic standards. In the new sports order, athletic performance is conditioned by the corporate values of teamwork and competition for media exposure. The amateur hero is replaced by the new sports system with the image of individualism projected by the exceptionally talented star who has been packaged for public consumption. Compared with the stellar amateur, needless to say, the publicly acclaimed superstar exemplifies the triumph of market, not inner values.

# 3

# From Commercialism to Corporate Athleticism: A Historical Perspective

Few would deny that intercollegiate athletics, especially competition between the so-called big powers in football and basketball, has fully emerged as a significant element in the sports entertainment offered weekly by national television networks, radio, and news media, and increasingly, by cable television networks. The expansion of major college sports events to the point where they have become important contributors to public entertainment is due in part to the development of the media in mass society. But what explains the intensification of athletic emphasis at institutions of higher learning in the first place? What provided the impetus for corporate athleticism?

Our synoptic review of intercollegiate athletics reveals identifiable links as early as the turn of the twentieth century between a growing, aggressive business system—with its free-for-all attitude toward winning at all costs—and the organization of intercollegiate athletics. University and college presidents were quick to see the financial potential of football. They were equally quick to realize the possibilities for recruiting additional students and the opportunities for forging close ties to the most dynamic element in American society, the business community.

Primarily because of brutalities and scandals, regulatory issues emerged surprisingly early in the history of intercollegiate athletics.[1] One realizes in retrospect that rampant commercialism and the scandals associated with big-time athletics are not unique to our time and circumstances.

While there is much that is similar, profound differences do exist in the organization and depth of contemporary links between sports and the business community. In part, these differences stem from the tightly integrated character of the current national economy, typified by large national corporations. But the large corporations are qualitatively different from earlier forms of business in their effect on the emergence of athleticism. This chapter traces the growth of athleticism, as well as deepens our understanding of those social structures that gave rise to corporate athleticism.

## The Early Days of College Sports

Committed largely to the academic life of students, the earliest American colleges cared little about the extracurricular aspects of student life. The earliest days of higher education were characterized by serious classes, studying, and of course religious devotion in chapel. Most students were educated for the ministry at Harvard, Yale, and later Princeton through a curriculum that included Latin, Greek, Hebrew, logic and rhetoric. Harvard's mission, articulated so eloquently in 1937 by Samuel Eliot Morrison, was to educate clergy "who would spell the difference between civilization and barbarism."[1] In this statement, Morrison captured both the spirit and the purpose of "higher" education in this country in its early days. He didn't mention college sports.

But this is not to say that sports did not exist at the early American colleges. Puritan goals of "keeping the spirit pure" formed one of the principal justifications for vigorous sports activities. Such activity would fatigue the body and thus enhance "pure living and pure thinking." Students were prompted, however, to train their wills and to become "moral athletes," to eschew those activities generally considered "low and unbecoming of gentlemen and scholars . . . "[2] But that was a bit much to ask, and students began to engage in recreational activities that ushered in the beginnings of intramuralism and led inevitably to intercollegiate competition.

As intramural teams were organized, the desire to test the mettle of teams from neighboring institutions grew. The evolution of campus sports as a club movement promoted and encouraged intercollegiate sports competition, and intercollegiate, rather than intramural, contests gained the greatest amount of student attention.

The historic moment occurred on August 3, 1852, when Harvard challenged and defeated Yale in a crew race on Lake Winnipesaukee in New Hampshire. This event was followed in 1859 by the first baseball game and in 1869 by the first intercollegiate football game in New Brunswick, New Jersey, between Rutgers and Princeton. By 1880 intercollegiate football, with its new rule changes and its first intercollegiate football association, set in motion the beginnings of the American game of football. William Baker, a noted sports historian, suggests that the contest between McGill University of Montreal and Harvard in 1874 was even more important in the development of the American game than was the "first" contest because of the introduction of rugby rules.[3] This change of rules and format not only delighted the spectators, it also provided the newly emergent game with what it needed to surpass in popularity the soccer-like game that was its forerunner. Who would have thought that this pastime invented to satisfy the physical needs of young men of breeding and taste would become the mass-entertainment spectacle it is today?

Even though the watershed of intercollegiate sports occurred with the first football contest, we should not lose sight of the significance of the attraction of crew, or boat races, to those well born. It surely was not lost to college administrators of the day, who were eager to capitalize on the excitement and the connection with competing schools. The relationship between the publicity generated by the races and increased admissions was something university presidents did not ignore. On this point, Joanna Davenport's speculation may be correct that these races inspired the practice of using sports to publicize a certain institution.[4] The belief that instant institutional fame and prestige accompanied athletic success was reinforced by the growing number of supporters of intercollegiate athletics. It did not take long for administrators to realize that people remembered the prowess of a school's athletic teams and its star performers and not the success of routine academic endeavors.[5]

But in the context of rapid demographic changes and dislocations, football overtook the more patrician sport of racing and emerged as the first of the major sports. Its popularity grew rapidly, and by the turn of the century it was becoming increasingly evident that football was the sport exceeding all others in its capacity to raise revenue. "King football," as it became known, was categorized as a major sport; those generating less money were labeled minor sports. These categories remain with us today, although they are now called, perhaps more accurately, revenue and nonrevenue sports.[6]

By the beginning of the twentieth century, the die had been cast. Football with its increasingly apparent links to commercialism was firmly launched as the principal intercollegiate sport. Frederick Rudolph described the sport thus: "Once the game had enlisted the support of alumni and administration, there was no stopping its growth. For once the *sport* had been accepted, the *games* had to be won.[7] Apparently, the launching of the game brought with it the belief that winning was also necessary.

The earliest years in the development of college football were marked not only by links with the business culture, but also by a heavy infusion of nationalism. In this environment, football actually acted as a stabilizing, unifying, and ultimately democratizing influence.[8] Between 1880 and 1910, new immigrants poured into the cities and towns of the industrial East and Midwest, creating in the process class and ethnic diversity; established inhabitants expressed considerable concern about the changing character of the urban society. Faced with a decline of ethnic homogeneity on college campuses, university and college administrators were prompted to use the integrative power of a successful athletic program. A winning football team, even in its earliest days, made it much easier for alumni and boosters to generate the funds needed to build additional athletic facilities and to restore a sense of collegiate unity that had been eroded by larger and more ethnically diversified student bodies and by the development of the elective curriculum.[9] Frederick Rudolph stated that "if every man did not take the same courses, at least he had an opportunity to cheer for the same team."[10]

The early twentieth century was a time of great social change, rapid urban and industrial growth, and increasing ethnic diversity. Under such circumstances, finding integrative symbols, especially those capturing the dynamic entrepreneurial spirit of the young nation, was no easy matter. Few articulated this association between sport and nationalism better than Theodore Roosevelt when he declared: "In any republic, courage is a prime necessity. . . . If one is to be a good citizen . . . athletics are good, especially in their rougher form, because they tend to develop such courage."[11]

Sacrifice and loyalty to national ideals were assumed to be part of the active commitment to sport and were highlighted in the work of Luther Gulick, an early twentieth-century leader in the recreation movement and an early contributor to American public administration theory. Gulick asserted that through the loyalty and self-sacrifice developed in team games, "we are laying the foundation for wider loyalty and a more discerning self-devotion to the great national ideals on which democracy rests."[12] So it was on sport generally, and in football specifically, that much of the weight of extending the unifying affective themes of American nationalism rested, a burden and a responsibility dubiously maintained even to this day.

## Football's Beginnings

An early indication of the future of intercollegiate sports was the rapidity and ease with which football became a fixture in university and campus life. It is instructive to recall how quickly the public seized upon the game (at the beginning more like a combination of soccer and rugby than the game familiar to millions of football fans today) with enthusiam and exhilaration. Universities and colleges immediately took advantage of this enormous popularity as a vehicle for attracting financial and political support from students, alumni, state legislators, and other prospective contributors. Unlike Cornell's President Andrew D. White, many university presidents were eager to meet opposing colleges on the gridiron in order to "agitate a bag of wind."[13] Apparently, "football as public relations to football as business would not, at some institutions, be much of a distance."[14]

Between 1880 and 1920, college football changed, reflecting more commercial, more "modern" values: secularism, equality of opportunity to compete, specialization and rationalization of roles, bureaucratic organization, quantification, and the quest for records.[15] These new characteristics were evident as early as the 1920s. Modern aspects of college sports can be seen in the changing role of football coaches and the growth of athletic establishments with their increasingly specialized personnel, and no coach exemplifies these changes better than Yale's legendary Walter Camp. It is difficult to imagine a better trailblazer for the newly emergent game of football than this remarkably gifted athlete who in four years as an undergraduate and two as a medical student competed in intercollegiate football, baseball, rowing, swimming, and track and field.[16]

Walter Camp must be regarded as the messenger of modernity to college sports. He carried his gifts as a versatile athlete into coaching to become an innovator in rules and tactics for football, and largely through his organizational genius the rough-and-tumble game of rugby gave birth to the distinctly American game of football. William Baker sees a connection between Camp's work as president of a clock manufacturing company and his imaginative revisions of some of the basic rules of rugby, rules which seemed to Camp disorderly and chaotic. Rugby's scrum, the progenitor of the modern football huddle, Camp thought to be not merely a chaotic mass of interlocked bodies, but an "unreasonable" way to try to move the ball down the field,[17] so he substituted what he thought to be "reasonable," well-planned tactics geared to achieve a well-coordinated momentum in moving the ball. As simple as this change may appear, one can easily imagine the kinds of changes it brought to the emerging game of football; consider for example the many times radio and televisions sports play-by-play announcers have commented on how a football team had moved with "clock-like precision" down the field in the waning moments of a game.

Through his organizational genius and innovative abilities, Camp created the model for the role of the head coach within a growing and increasingly complex sports system. The development of specific roles, a hallmark of bureaucratic development in any hierarchical organization, can also be traced at the team sports level to Walter Camp. For the first time, the actual training of "specialists" began to occur. Under Camp, the head coach's responsibilities at Yale were extended to include central authority over the administration of specific sporting activities.[18] Camp contributed to the establishment of the formal rules of the game, and he introduced a record-keeping system and bureaucracy for the sport by maintaining extensive records on team formation and training method, a practice that contributed to the standardization of procedures and ensured the continuity of the game. Although college football in Camp's day was different in some respects from its modern counterpart, there is a clear line from Camp's initial methods and procedures to those of the most highly developed and specialized football organization existing today.[19]

Walter Camp's methods caught on, and before long, the introduction of other administrative innovations suggesting a growing integration of management values and techniques into college football. As athletic programs continued to expand, university administrators established centrally appointed athletic committees to promote the new values of efficiency and control. Program growth, expanding financial activities, and growing central authority over the administration and management, along with growing alumni insistence on a winning program, established a pattern that remains the model for the modern athletic complex. One result of these changes was that the alumni were integrated into the evolving college sports system.[20]

## Football's Growing Pains and Emerging Regulation

Like the game itself, the development of football was full of fits and starts. The game also absorbed its share of public criticism, leveled especially at its evident brutality. In 1905 alone, 18 athletes died and nearly 150 were injured in collegiate football games. The growing national press, eager for the sensational, seized upon such news, producing a public outcry for the abolishment of football. The outcry was so great that President Theodore Roosevelt himself intervened. In his typical manner of dealing with corruption in public and private life, he called the principals together for lunch at the White House and directed them to clean up the game. The principals in this case were representatives from Harvard, Yale, and Princeton. They responded accordingly by holding a national conference that led to the founding of the first association for the regulation of college athletics: the Intercollegiate Athletic Association (ICAA), later to become the National Collegiate Athletic Association (NCAA).[21] Charged with adopting rules and procedures that would lead to the reduction, if not elimination, of brutality, the formation of the ICAA temporarily muted the criticisms directed at intercollegiate athletics.

By the 1920s there was no returning to a more informal game. College football was fast becoming a "national mania" and its future would be linked with the development of mass entertainment in a growing industrial society. With this growth came "new freedoms, new drives, new searchings for emotional and physical outlets; and sports seemed to provide the one big national denominator."[22] This so-called Golden Era of college sports was a time of stadium building, a time in which universities and colleges engaged in a large-scale construction program of building sport complexes to accommodate growing spectator interest. Yale built a seventy-five-thousand seat stadium, at that time the nation's largest.[23] In 1923 the University of Michigan built a field house large enough to contain a football game.[24] Almost ninety thousand screaming spectators could watch their favorite team parade onto the gridiron at Ann Arbor by 1927, and twenty-one years later a modern $4 million football stadium would be built with the profits from the gate receipts alone, a tradition which continues at Michigan.[25]

On the West Coast, gigantic sports arenas were built in Los Angeles and Pasadena in anticipation of the continued growth of spectator interest. The glitter and glamour of the Roaring Twenties was reflected by the color and imaginative spectacle of big marching bands, majorettes, and that special esprit and reckless abandon captured today by Keith Jackson and other "color" commentators on Saturday football games. Truly, as William Baker suggests, the foundations of modern football were laid in the 1920s.[26]

During this time, increasing numbers of football stadia were not the only evidence of growing fan interest. The amount of money being spent by fans on recreational activities was also increasing. The gate receipts of forty-nine major colleges increased from $2,696,345 to over $9,000,000 from 1921 to 1929. Attendance for the same period more than doubled from 1,504,319 to 3,617,421.[27] By 1929, the year the bottom fell out of the stock market, an estimated twenty million people a year were attending college football games.[28]

College athletics was also affected by a little-publicized series of events that amounted to formal recognition that intercollegiate athletics had actually become a part of higher education and that they could hardly be perceived any longer as extracurricular. For example, the 1920s gave birth to athletic dormitories, professional trainers, and full-time athletic coaches, all part of what we have come to recognize as the infrastructure of big-time college athletics. These changes allowed sports programs to grow and opened opportunities for these programs to gain institutional funds. Add to this the continuing growth of alumni associations that increasingly identified themselves with their colleges through sports and the institutionalization of college athletics was all but complete.

## Commercialism and College Athletics

Not everyone was impressed by the millions of fans and dollars. Alarmed by the growing commercialism and abuses in recruitment in college athletics, the prestigious Carnegie Foundation issued a report on the situation in 1929. Known as the Carnegie Report on American College Athletics, the study condemned the "paid coach, the gate receipts, the special training," and declared that football was no longer a student's game. Instead, the report called it "a highly organized commercial enterprise," and referred to "professional coaches" and to administrators who "take a slice of the profits for college buildings."[29] The foundation was quite clear regarding responsibility for correcting the situation: "The defense of the intellectual integrity of the college and university lies with the president and faculty."[30]

The Carnegie Report was received with a predictable lack of enthusiasm. Although there was a decline in the recruiting and subsidizing of college athletics following the report's publication, it seems in retrospect to have been due primarily to the effects of the crippling depression and the threat of a major war. Like so many reports gathering dust on library shelves, this one was mostly ignored, except by an occasional scholar and even more occasional reformer.[31] One reason for the Carnegie Report's negligible effect on commercialism in college sports was the existence of a formidable sports clientele—groups that for business and commercial purposes found the promotion of college athletics, especially football, indispensable to their welfare. By the end of the first quarter of the twentieth century, a strong and well-defined sports business network had already emerged and taken on formidable shape.

Perhaps there is a lesson to be learned from history. In spite of repeated efforts to eradicate abuses associated with college sports, it is unlikely that much can be done to correct abuses as long as powerful business connections exist among those who profit from the continuation of college athletics in its present commercial forms. In effect, the basis for greater alumni influence in college sports already existed in the 1920s. In the period up to and including the Savage Report, however, many of the connections were symbolic and not fully realized materially. The alumni in earlier areas could not know the political-economic implications of their intense emotional attachments to their universities' sports programs; contemporary alumni and boosters consciously use their financial resources to lobby not merely for the retention but for the expansion of sports programs. Recent news stories indicating the depth of booster involvement both in the recruiting and retention of top-flight college athletes suggest that more is required to rid the system of such abuses than the official ranting and raving we have become so accustomed to hearing.

## From Commercialism to Corporate Athleticism— the 1930s to the 1950s

The Great Depression and World War II slowed the rapid growth of college athletics by reducing their budgets. Extracurricular activities were curtailed and athletic contests had to be rescheduled to save travel costs. In retrospect, these adjustments seem merely to have delayed the commercial emphasis in college athletics. For example, the liberation of player substitution rules in the late 1940s actually required an expansion in the size of athlete rosters, and abuses in recruiting, even for reduced athletic machines, continued unabated.[32]

By the early 1950s the NCAA belatedly recognized the problem of commercialism in college sports, so emphatically referred to in the 1929 Carnegie Report, by officially authorizing the use of athletic grants-in-aid. The rationale for doing so was that not only would this policy be realistic, but it would also enable the NCAA to extend its regulatory influence over recruiting practices. In addition, the proponents of this policy extending the NCAA's rule asserted, the Alice-in-Wonderland logic notwithstanding, that granting athletic scholarships and increasing regulatory control would bring about "parity" among the competing institutions and would thereby preserve the amateur status of athletes and the existing system of college athletics.[33] Given the growth of commercialism in college athletics, with all of its associated abuses, one can reasonably question the motivation behind and the intent of these rules. Surely the NCAA's attempt to regulate the recruitment process was not naive; it may well have been motivated by an eagerness to create the appearance of bringing order to a sports system nearly out of control.

Obviously, the NCAA's role in regulating the recruitment of college athletes has been less than a success. One need only look at the growing list of rule violators among the most competitive institutions for evidence of its failure. To give just one example, in 1984 the University of Florida was granted the dubious distinction of being charged with violating more NCAA rules than any university in the NCAA's history. In the more than thirty years since the NCAA adopted its grants-in-aid policy, the business and commercial aspects of college sports, especially in football and basketball at Division I-A institutions, have enhanced neither the return to amateurism nor university control of college sports. We take up the matter of the NCAA's ability to regulate recruitment violations in considerable detail in chapter 6.

Despite the NCAA's efforts, by the 1950s commercialization had developed to the point that football and basketball players had become commodities in a growing mass entertainment industry, one that now includes the many of the leading universities in the United States. The "scholarship" system was the means by which to procure these players. To obtain scarce athletic talent, universities increased financial "assistance," aided especially by alumni and boosters, who mobilized their efforts to get the best recruits. The circumvention of newly formulated NCAA rules became a business calculation: a felt necessity, worth taking risks for.

Minimal as they were, the NCAA limitations on the granting of athletic scholarships did affect the bargaining power of competing institutions and thus in some ways encouraged the more aggressive tactics of alumni; some booster groups were tempted to resort to under-the-table payments and "slush funds" in order to attract athletes who could make the difference between winning and losing. In athletic scholarships we see the origins of the underground economy discussed in chapter 5.

## TV and Corporate Athleticism— the 1960s to the 1970s

The 1960s and 1970s were a period of extraordinary growth for sports entertainment in the United States. Although many expected professional sports franchises to saturate the country with sports spectacles, few predicted that college and university sports programs would also join the business of providing "major league" contests.[34] Crucial to this latest sports explosion was the emergence of television as the most potent medium of mass communication. If television was the medium, then mass entertainment was to become the message, with football and later basketball to become its texts.

The effect of television on the development of commercialism in intercollegiate sport is complex, and certain aspects of that development require closer examination. Television does more than perpetuate the marriage of the mass media to sports spectacles; it has fundamentally changed and reordered the business framework in which athleticism takes place. It has widened the marketing of the product and at the same time has begun a restructuring of the sports marketplace itself. Equally important, it has supplanted the sanctions associated with NCAA rules.

Television is the main producer of sports entertainment, and in this capacity, it strengthens the corporate side of big-time, competitive intercollegiate athletics by defining the terms in which market competition takes place. Only the most naive would assume that efforts to gain national rankings and television exposure, regardless of the cost of getting there, are not the prime motivating forces in big-time college sports. Television has introduced commercialism of a new kind into college sports. What is different about contemporary commercialism in intercollegiate sports is the extensive character and organization of market capitalism as we approach the twenty-first century. We have moved from the pre-1929, relatively unregulated business system to the planned organization of corporate institutions and to the more regulated, integrated arrangement of business systems.

In some respects, the consequences for universities and colleges able to compete for the "positional goods" of national rank and television revenues are not very different from what we have observed in the past. The competitors themselves have changed; that is, there are fewer "private" institutions able to compete in football for national honors in Division I-A, although this is less true in the case of basketball at the Division I-A level.

## The Black Athlete and the Development of Corporate Athleticism

While great black athletes did play college football as early as the turn of this century, they are notable almost as much for their small numbers on white campuses as they are for their exceptional talent. William H. Lewis at Amherst (who played during the years 1890–93), Fritz Pollard at Brown (1915–19), Paul Robeson at Rutgers (1917–21), and Fred "Duke" Slater at Iowa (1918–21) come instantly to mind. But the full emergence of the black athlete on the national scene had to wait until after World War II for the historic Supreme Court decision of 1954 outlawing racial segregation in the public schools. During the 1940s and 1950s, Woody Strode, Kenny Washington, and Jackie Robinson started a tradition of black athletes at UCLA that continues in southern California today.

Since 1954 a revolution has been going on. One result has been the emergence of, and in some sports virtual domination by, black athletes; NCAA Division I-A intercollegiate basketball perhaps most dramatically illustrates this black dominance. After years of having almost no blacks in athletics, the Southwest and Southeast Conferences became well represented by black performers. The University of Texas added six black football players between 1963 and 1973; the University of Mississippi, having achieved notoriety for refusing James Meredith entrance to its classrooms in 1962, added five during these years; and the University of Alabama, previously best known for Governor George C. Wallace's personally blocking its doors to prevent the entrance of black students, added thirteen blacks to its athletic teams.[35] Ironically, the university (probably) had to pay the black athletes to get them to come. And the University of Pittsburgh, a center for football talent and the producer of the Dallas Cowboys' All-Pro running back Tony Dorsett, went from two to thirty-one black football players during the same period.[36]

Universities have reaped financial gains from high-visibility, revenue-generating sports of football and basketball, sports in which blacks are disproportionately represented, but they have gained further advantages through their uneven exchange with athletes in other ways as well. Black athletes constitute the lifeblood of major collegiate football and basketball powers. In fact, the dominance of black basketball players is all but total among the strongest teams. Georgetown University is a case in point. In a 1984 game, Georgetown, rated as the nation's best quintet in the early part of the 1984–85 season, played the University of Nevada, Las Vegas, on Georgetown's home court in Washington, D.C. At times all ten players on the court were black, in contrast with the virtually all-white student body of Georgetown cheering their magnificent team on to victory from the stands.

In spite of what they have to offer, black athletes still receive fewer than one in ten of the athletic scholarships given out in the United States. Of those fortunate few who do receive scholarships, approximately 65 percent to 75 percent are not likely to graduate, and of those who do, 75 percent will graduate with degrees in physical education, the acceptable "jock major," which is seldom good preparation for the hard knocks for life after sports.[37]

Harry Edwards, arguably the best authority on the subject of the exploitation of black athletes, has drawn attention to the inadequate compensation often awarded to black athletes. According to Edwards, it is not the athletes who have failed to live up to their part of the bargain; rather, it is higher education which has failed to compensate athletes appropriately for showcasing the universities' high-visibility programs. Universities have benefited directly in the form of huge gate receipts, donors to university programs, television revenues, and national visibility (and what president won't jump at the opportunity to advertise his university during those halftime breaks in the game).[38]

The increasing recruitment of black athletes began as the mass media was transforming much of the financial and economic structure of intercollegiate athletics. With its growing audience appeal, television was increasing the size of the markets for the entertainment products of universities, and thus was directly contributing to the recruitment and exploitation of the paid gladiators hired by institutions to do one thing: perform.

So blacks fully emerged on the national athletic scene in many of the major colleges and universities at a time when the mass media was beginning to change profoundly the social character of entertainment in the United States. Powerful institutional forces, outside and within black communities, were laying the groundwork for the recruitment and development of an essential commodity, prime athletic talent.

## Women's Athletics and the Development of Corporate Athleticism

Our focus in this chapter is on those forces that have shaped commercialism and corporatism in the development of intercollegiate athletics, and in this context, women's sports programs have received little of our attention because until recently they remained strongholds of amateurism and intramuralism scarcely noticed by nonparticipants and almost invisible to alumni and boosters.[39] The early mainstays of women's sports on campus had been croquet, walking, ice skating, and later tennis, basketball, volleyball, field hockey, track and field, swimming, and gymnastics. There was little change in the attitude toward women's sports until the historic passage in 1972 of Title IX, which required colleges and universities to provide women with opportunities in athletics equal to those extended to men. Title IX was manifestly clear that there should be no sex discrimination in any educational institution receiving federal funds. What was not so clear was how women's programs could be supported without curtailing the men's programs. Sensing a danger to money-making sports, the NCAA sued in order to have the revenue-producing sports exempted from Title IX requirements.[40]

Fearing adverse effects on the ability of major athletic powers to recruit star athletes for their growing programs, the NCAA sought initially to thwart the effect of Title IX. Having failed to do so, the NCAA recently took over the championship events for women's athletics from the Association for Intercollegiate Athletics for Women (AIAW), just at a time when the potential revenue growth and women athletes themselves may become valuable assets to their institutions as money-making attractions.[41] More recently, women's athletics suffered a setback when the courts ruled that Athletic programs not receiving federal funds are exempt from Title IX antidiscrimination provisions.[40]

The full development of corporate athleticism in women's sports teams lies in the future. But already the inevitable signs are appearing of recruiting "abuses" associated almost exclusively up until now with highly competitive men's athletics. These abuses are occurring at a time when television is creating, as it did with the international attraction of Olympic gymnastics, new markets for athleticism of all kinds, so it seems likely that women's athletics may eventually become the object of television's exposure and development. Women's athletics has come a long way from clubhouse intramuralism, and it will go far as its attractiveness is communicated to larger audiences through the mass media.

## Conclusion

This historical overview of the commercial aspects of intercollegiate sports reveals several factors that have influenced the present bureaucratic, and corporate character of college sports. The structure of intercollegiate athletics was altered by changing socioeconomic forces that shaped the features of newly commercialized athletics and defined the recreational needs of students and spectators alike.

At the same time, a new set of values reflecting the growing ascendancy of corporate values and norms was being forged in mass society. Within this context record keeping took shape as the standard of excellence and of the "naturalness" of the market model of competition—a model whose cultural corollary is an emphasis on skill acquisition as a condition of fun and personal development.[42]

It is also within this context of changing values that the complex and growing system of corporate athleticism developed, a system that increasingly demanded both bureaucratic structures and enhanced specificity of the roles within them. In this context the certified and thoroughly professional coach became organizer, manager, and entrepreneur. Numerous rule changes making college sports more appealing to wider publics took place. Concomitant with this synthesis of market and bureaucratic norms was the formidable ability of the market, via television, to penetrate the popular consciousness.

We have noted the popularity of intercollegiate football from its beginnings and the rapidity with which the game was absorbed by universities and colleges and by the public. The incorporation of a mass public into the structures of sports-induced market forces is a pattern that we recognize only too clearly today. In this way, the development of modern sport generally, and intercollegiate football specifically, is at the same time constitutive of and separate from the social context existing at a given time.[43] While we shall not try to explain the entire development of intercollegiate football by a crude Marxist analysis, we believe that market capitalism and its transition to more bureaucratic structures has significantly influenced the historical evolution of college sports from amateurism to corporate athleticism as the dominant organizing mode for big-time college athletics. What the history of commercialism in sports reveals, in short, is the extraordinary reduction of athletics to a limited set of values and beliefs derived primarily from the market system. The emphasis on technique and role differentiation in football, developed initially by Walter Camp, can be seen as an attempt to integrate "scientific" play and "amateurism." As we shall argue in more detail, amateurism is incompatible with the market system, with its subjugation of all organized activity to a rational model of productive efficiency. The attitudes resulting from this productive process were powerful enough that they were able to transform narrow, class-specific responses into the broader, shared cultural experiences that now predominate in mass society.

## Notes

1. Samuel Eliot Morison, *Harvard College in the Seventeenth Century* (Cambridge: Harvard University Press, 1937), p. 6.

2. Ralph Barton Perry, *Puritanism and Democracy* (New York: Vanguard, 1944), 245.

3. William J. Baker, *Sports in the Modern World* (Totowa, NJ: Rowman and Littlefield, 1982), 128.

4. Joanna Davenport, "From Crew to Commercialism—The Paradox of Sport in Higher Education" (Paper presented at the Conference on Sports and Higher Education, Skidmore College, March, 1983), 5.

5. Sanborn Gove Tenney, "Athletics at Williams," *Outing* 17 (1890):142.

6. Leroy Ervin and Sue McCaffrey, "Intercollegiate Football and Higher Education, 1880–1980: A Century of Growth, Commercialization, and Conflict" (Paper presented at the Conference on Sports and Higher Education" Skidmore College, March, 1983), 5.

7. D.S. Eitzen and G. Sage, *Sociology of American Sport* (Dubuque, Iowa: William C. Brown Co., 1978), 72.

8. Frederick Rudolph, *The American College and University: A History* (New York: Vintage Books, 1962), 379.

9. Davenport, "From Crew to Commercialism," 6.

10. Rudolph, *The American College,* 381.

11. Alexander M. Weyand, *The Sage of American Football Development* (New York: Macmillan, 1955), viii–ix.

12. Luther Gulick, *A Philosophy of Play* (New York: Charles Scribner's Sons, 1920), 262.

13. Kent Sagendorph, *Michigan: The Story of the University* (New York: 1948), 150, cited in Rudolph, *The American College,* 374.

14. Rudolph, *The American College,* 386.

15. Allen Guttman, *From Ritual to Record: The Nature of Modern Sports* (New York: Columbia University Press, 1978), 16.

16. Baker, *Sports in the Modern World,* 129.

17. Ibid.

18. Ervin and McCaffey, 9.

19. Ibid.

20. Rudolph, *The American College,* 382–84; John Savage, *American College Athletics* (New York: The Carnegie Foundation, 1929), 23–24.

21. Guy L. Lewis, "Theodore Roosevelt's Role in the 1905 Football Controversy," *Research Quarterly* 40 (December 1969):717–24.

22. Rudolph, *The American College,* 382.

23. Ervin and McCaffey, 15.

24. Rudolph, *The American College,* 381.

25. Ibid., 389.

26. Baker, *Sports in the Modern World,* 217.

27. Ervin and McCaffey, 15.

28. W. Freeman, "College Athletics in the Twenties: The Golden Age or Fool's Gold." (Paper presented at History Symposium of the National Association for Sport and Physical Education, Seattle, Wash., April 1977). Cited in Joanna Davenport, "From Crew to Commercialism," 9.

29. John Savage, *American College Athletics,* viii.

30. Ibid., xx.

31. Ervin and McCaffey, 17.

32. Ibid.

33. Ibid., 18.

34. Baker, *Sports in the Modern World,* 318.

35. Gregory S. Sojka, "The Evolution of the Student-Athlete in America: From Divinity to the Divine" (Paper presented at the Conference on Sports and Higher Education, Skidmore College, March 1982), 12.

36. Kenneth Denlinger and Leonard Shapiro, *Athletes for Sale* (New York: Thomas Y. Crowell, 1975), 33.

37. Harry Edwards, "Educating Black Athletes," *The Atlantic Monthly* (August 1983):31–38.

38. Ibid.

39. Sojka, "The Education of the Student-Athlete," 15.

40. Davenport, "From Crew to Commercialism," 21.

41. Sojka, "The Education of the Student-Athlete," 17.

42. Richard Grunneau, *Class, Sports, and Social Development* (Amherst, Mass.: The University of Massachusetts Press, 1983), 143.

43. Ibid., 140.

# 4
# The Media and the Transformation of College Sports

S tartling as it may seem, approximately 98 percent of all homes in the United States own television sets. In the typical American home, the television is on for more than six and a half hours a day, and over 40 percent of the free time of most Americans is spent in front of this mesmerizing machine.[1] Television viewing accounts for three-quarters of all of the time Americans devote to the mass media. This means that when we speak of mass media, for all practical purposes we mean television, and television for all practical purposes means entertainment. As such, television forms an important mechanism for adding cultural accretions—in other words, television provides access to instant enjoyment and acts as an agent of cultural change—to mass postindustrial societies like the United States.

In many ways television as a medium is just too big and too easily wired into the American collective consciousness to be inspected as if it were a mere artifact of modern culture. Television is a popular art as well as a social force, which makes it doubly difficult to make pronouncements about what it produces.

We argue in this book that television has in fact replaced universities and colleges as the producer of intercollegiate sports. The medium is not only a "producer's" medium, but in our view a male producer's medium as well. The implications of this situation are important for a general understanding of the medium and for our analysis of the commercial development of intercollegiate athletics.

Perhaps the most interesting and most demanding aspects of television stem from the complex ways that television seems to be intertwined with the culture that provides a context which in turn is reflected in its very programming. It certainly is the primary means of public communication in the United States, and as a result it constitutes that part of the culture shared most by the entire population. If television is the primary means of public communication, and we think it is, then to talk about what we as a culture share is to talk about what we are.

Television's audience is made up of Americans differentiated by age, sex, life-style, and buying power for advertisers. This fact helps us understand some of the trends in programming and why perhaps someone's favorite program has been cancelled as a result of the latest popularity ratings. Yesterday's fans of the popular detective show "Mod Squad" are today's fans of the more mature "Hill Street Blues." But curiously enough, sports fans seem to be "immune" to changes in age, life-style, and buying power. It seems to us that part of the great power of sports programming on television stems from early fantasy development that remains essentially intact in later life. Perhaps this is just another way of saying that after all is said and done the vast televiewing public seems to accept the medium on its own terms and as a reflection of itself, to the consternation of those who try to find fault with the medium.

Finally, we are intrigued with a point often missed when television programming and audiences are discussed and analyzed: television programming seems to be the medium through which the most cherished myths in American culture (myths such as the ultimate triumph of good over evil, the inevitable success of hard work and fair play, the Horatio Alger myth) have found enduring expression. Sports, we contend, captures much of this popular cultural expression, and this explains why large audiences will sit hour after hour, week after week, and watch essentially the same stories and myths acted out repeatedly either in television "drama" or in sports. In fact, we believe that televised sports has become that cultural hearth where "real" drama occurs in postindustrial America.

Cultural myths, whether expressed in television drama or in sports, constitute the organizing "principle" of American society and thus the organizing principle of television as well. As a result, neither television drama nor sports should be dismissed as trivial. What television reveals is a profound circularity between primordial cultural norms and the medium through which they are produced. McLuhan was right; the medium is the message.

This chapter analyzes how this most pervasive of media translates sports activities into its own medium and through its own mechanisms, influencing the very definition of what constitutes sport. In other words, television produces the perceptions that define sports standards. It does this because it, not universities and colleges, is the ultimate producer of college sports.

## Media and Shifts in Time Use in the United States

Since the 1930s a major shift has occurred in how Americans use their time, especially their recreation or leisure time; the introduction of television after World War II seems to be an obvious explanation for this change.[2] Although studies of how humans allocate time have their methodological problems, they can be extremely useful in revealing fundamental changes in the effects of technology on mass populations, and these studies reveal discernable patterns indicating that something profound has happened in the ways in which Americans use their leisure time.

Since the end of World War II, much leisure time has been focused on such things as visiting friends and relatives, organizational activity (usually this means church attendance), moonlighting, and watching television.[3] As early as the mid-sixties, studies indicated that Americans were devoting as many as two hours a day, seven days a week, to TV watching, their favorite pastime, and that nearly one-third of all leisure time available to adults was used for recreational activity.[4] It has been estimated that these changes were accomplished at the expense of such recreational activities as listening to the radio, reading, going to the movies, attending live sporting events and the theater, as well as the more traditional activities of visiting friends, driving, playing cards, and so forth.[5] The underlying reason for these changes in leisure time activities seems to be television. It alone is responsible for changing a homogenous culture as it revolutionizes contemporary American life.

## Sports Activity and Leisure Time Use

Any doubt that sports are the preferred form of entertainment on television should be dispelled by a recent national survey.[6] For example, most of the respondents surveyed expressed what the report termed a "high interest" in watching sports events. Nearly three out of four (73 percent) watch or listen to sports news; 60 percent talked with friends about sports; and 58 percent read the sports pages of their daily newspaper regularly.[7] Not too surprisingly, and significantly for this study, football, basketball, baseball, and gymnastics were the preferred objects of spectator interest.[8]

Reading such surveys carefully reveals something else. Spectatorship seems to be linked in a circular way to participation in sports and to ardent fan interest. For example, this same survey indicates that seven of ten Americans fourteen years and older are engaged in one or more sports-related activities (viewing televised sports, listening to sports, reading and/or talking about sports) at least once a day. Most are men who tend to be better educated and who live (not surprisingly) in larger American cities. Similarly, there is mounting evidence that increasing numbers of Americans are not only sports watchers but are sports participants as well.[9]

The fact that so many Americans express a high degree of interest in sports participation should come as no surprise, given the popularity of "workout" books written and promoted by such entertainment notables as Jane Fonda, Victoria Principal, and the effervescent Richard Simmons. While much of this sports activity is associated with younger groups, men, and the generally well-to-do, other groups seem to be included in the sports and fitness fad that has developed in the United States. Women, older people, and minorities have joined the national sports parade, and interestingly, there seem to be few differences in attitudes toward sports participation between whites and blacks.

The significance of this is clear. We are witnessing a fundamental change in how more and more Americans are spending their leisure time. Instead of using time to improve their minds by reading more books, or to pursue neighborly activities, Americans increasingly are participating in a leisure time industry that has television at its center.

## The Expansion of Cable Television

In this section we will focus attention on some of the factors that have contributed to the further expansion of cable television networks and then relate that expansion to the main argument of this chapter: that television has become the real producer of sports generally and big-time intercollegiate sports specifically. The question to be answered here is how recent developments in television affect this situation.

Just as broadcast television began to change fundamentally the character of the mass media in the United States in the early 1950s, cable television is now changing what we expect from television in the years to come.[10] Although cable television predates the 1950s when it served primarily rural communities, its growth has been nothing less than extraordinary in the last ten years; this growth has been due largely to the relaxation of government regulation and to the extended use of communications satellites by private businesses.[11] The 1970s was a decade of rapid expansion of cable systems, because the Federal Communications Commission (FCC) relaxed regulatory constraints and because the launching of space satellites opened many opportunities to commercial investors.[12] As we shall see, the world of corporate video would never be the same.

In 1975, Time, Inc. established the first national network to distribute cable programs to local operators. Since then, more than twenty-eight million people have become cable users, with approximately twenty-five thousand being added every month. It is estimated that over 34 percent of the homes in the United States currently receive cable, and one-half will have access to it in the future.[13]

But how has this change affected the use of television as the prime producer for college sports? Cable differs from broadcast television (network television) in several ways. Cable offers its viewers more expanded channel capacity and two-way communication; it can also be coupled with other communication technologies, for example, newspapers, radio, film, books, and even still pictures.[14] Cable's expanded capacities interest us because with expanded channel capacity comes more specialized television production. This is why the first all-sports channels, movie channels, weather channels, and so forth, can exist on cable and not on broadcast television.

Anyone who thinks that cable television is a fly-by-night phenomenon, think again. The recent profusion of new networks indicates otherwise. According to one report, more than fifty-one national satellite-distributed cable networks have appeared in the last ten years, including three all-news channels, two all-sports channels, four religious networks, a Spanish-speaking network, and others that vie for what promises to be an increasingly larger market.[15]

Another indicator of the permanency of cable network television comes from the growth of cable TV's market share, gained largely at the expense of the established broadcast networks. In 1979, in some areas of the United States, the established broadcast networks (CBS, NBC, and ABC) earned only 70 percent of the television market and a 92 percent overall share nationally. In 1981 the big three got only 81 percent of the national market.[16] These facts suggest a remarkable growth in and challenge by a part of the industry that, like Topsy, has just "growed" in the last ten years.

Most important, cable systems will soon be able to deliver programs at a low marginal cost per additional channel, while established broadcast networks will continue to offer what the industry calls one "page," program, at a time. Cable operators can presently offer fifty "pages" or more simultaneously. Their only concern are the ability to buy programming for broadcast and not having to face direct competitors with the same production capabilities. Should such competition develop, however, it is likely that consumers will reap the advantages by having several producers of television entertainment to choose among.

Earlier we suggested that cable networks seemed to be seeking advertisers in order to meet growing costs of production. Another factor increasing the need for advertising revenues exists. With more specialized programming, we should expect that broadcast franchises will decrease in value. As the viewer audience is fractured into smaller and smaller groups, there will be less incentive for advertisers to invest at the same levels as in the past, and a shortfall in advertising revenues will result. The money will have to be made up from somewhere.

The importance of the role of advertising is often neglected in many discussions of television. Too often focus is on the actual televised program, and this conveniently shields the economic and social importance of advertising as the delivery system of commodities. The media is more accurately viewed as a delivery system for advertising. According to Jerry Mander, a former advertising executive, the best way to think of advertising is as a system designed to purvey what people don't need," a system that separates people from direct fulfillment, and "teaches" that satisfaction occurs only through the purchase of commodities purveyed by the media.[17]

New forms of advertisement are appearing at the same time that television production becomes more specialized.[18] For example, advertisers are beginning to "sponsor" programs as showcases for their products. Companies like Bristol-Myers will act as both producer and main distributor for beauty-care programs. Health- and exercise-related shows will be sponsored by products that purport to promote better health through exercise. The list can go on and on, but the point is clear. As the targeting of groups becomes a factor in programming decisions, television advertisers will increasingly become the program producers. This is just as true for advertisers of products that have no logical connection with a given activity, but have through years of advertising and promotion become associated in the public mind with an activity or pastime. Beer and sports, especially sports like football, baseball, and basketball, have become inseparable, and this explains why such firms as Anheuser-Busch are beginning to experiment and invest in sports programming through local and regional cable networks. For the purposes of this discussion, one should keep in mind that the two biggest entertainment draws on cable continue to be sports and movies. These areas were also the first to be developed for national audiences.[19] Might Ted Turner's "superstation" WTBS be nothing less than a prototype for the future of mass entertainment in the United States? The so-called bottom line is "what will people pay for?" The answer apparently is sports and movies.[20]

Without appearing to be too facile in predicting the future of television, we think that there exists considerable agreement that cable and its related technologies will contribute to make profound changes in what the American viewing public will be exposed to in the near future. Such innovations as large, multichannel cable systems, low-power TV (permitting closer geographic use of the same broadcast frequencies), direct-broadcast services, and fiber-optic networks that can exceed multichannel capacities using the coaxial cable, will do what some suggest by increasing the number of television broadcast channels.[21] These innovations suggest that the American viewing public will have more television packages to consume and moreover that the economic premises governing the behavior of the existing, large broadcast networks will very likely be fundamentally changed.

In the past (and to a large extent today), the largest television networks attempted to produce entertainment packages appealing to the largest audiences possible. This strategy was induced by a built-in incentive system that caused advertisers to focus on selling goods and services having national appeal. As television audiences grew in size, so did the costs of buying time on networks, and this circular relationship kept the system economically viable. But all of this may be changing significantly. As new, national cable systems continue to grow and challenge the established networks, they will provide local entrepreneurs an opportunity to make better bargains and further differentiate the market.

While most will agree that we are witnessing a telecommunications revolution, some believe that for political and economic reasons we are in for more of the same kinds of programming that the networks have always provided, primarily because the same forces that control broadcast television will in the long run control cable's development as well. The key to more decentralized programming in the future in the United States is a matter of "access." It may even be too late to offset the growing concentration of the "means of communication corporate domination" that continues from the last fifty years of media ownership.[22] What is at stake is the shape and perception of a society dominated by corporate power and the products that are its lifeblood. The existing system depends on mass audiences, and one can assume that those who presently "own" the system will not accept challenges to that control without a fight.

In conclusion, the recent and rapid development of cable networks has introduced the issue of scale into the development of sports markets. That is to say, cable television has further expanded what the established networks have begun: it is providing increased opportunities for the telecasting of sports and is developing in the process new and innovative ways of enhancing the financial role of advertisers. What does all of this mean for the future? In the short run we can expect that technological expansion, coupled with new ways of presenting products to larger and more "targeted" sports audiences, will further alter how viewers perceive sports.

## Television and Sports

How does television affect sports? How does the operation of sports enhance the integrative mechanisms within a society like that of the United States? In this section we attempt to delineate some of the relationships between television and sports. Specific attention will be given to those features of television that particularly enhance the visible and dramatic effects of sports as a competitive contest and thus make sports attractive to large spectator markets. Given that 98 percent of the homes in the United States now possess television sets, TV's potential as a mechanism for the remolding of old values and the diffusion of new values within American society seems clear. Television, as we shall demonstrate, is the mobilizing force that has shaped the foundations for the evolution of sports to a new stage of corporate organization, for the presentation of sports on television helps to integrate more fully the profit motive into the organization of intercollegiate sports. It is in this and other ways that television has guided the restructuring of sports to its present institutional forms.

## Television's Social Power

Television's great power lies in its ability to create new symbols and personalities and bring the viewer into a more intimate acquaintance with the images presented. In general, television brings individuals into contact with many events, images, and life experiences, and at the same time, it fosters a sense of excitement or active involvement on the part of the viewer. Its particular power is that it creates expectations and vicarious images.[23] Its most insidious effect is that it conditions the total communication environment in which people exist and structures the ways in which viewers respond to its presentation of dramatic events.

At the same time, and more critically, television portrays only a limited range of human emotions, perplexities, and situations. That this may be due to the inherent properties of television is an interesting question, but it is not one that will be dealt with at length here. It seems to us that although there may be "technical" limitations in television that may in some ways affect the character and substance of what is communicated, the trivial character of television is more a result of its corporate character. As long as producers at some companies want to reach the largest audience possible for the least amount of investment, they will tend to design television programming to "appeal" to the largest targeted groups.[24]

On the cultural level, television helps to shape the language of discourse by its very topicality and to make society more homogenous by creating a nonrepresentative, nonconcrete, and imaged world for a national audience.[25] One gets the impression traveling from city to city that Americans ask the same questions of one another: "Who won?" And "Who is sleeping with whom on the soaps?"

Finally, television does more than create new needs to be fulfilled and new goods to consume; it also holds the commodity system together. As a commodity itself, it gives the commodity system a boost when it is purchased. Television creates opportunities for experience that can be had by large segments of the American population almost simultaneously. This reduction of experience has political and social implications. First, it makes it much easier for corporate advertisers to design and control advertising and to control further the confined channel existence that is becoming a disturbing reality of American social life.[26]

## Television's Social Power and the Creation of New Markets

How is TV working as the principal instrument to reshape the American sociocultural landscape? Basically, it is through TV's ability to structure social options, enforce social norms, and author expectations, values, and standards of judgments that Americans apply to life. We agree with David Altheide and Robert Snow that "the media are powerful because people have adopted a media logic, that is, a knowledge framework which serves both as guidelines for the formation of ideas as well as interpretations and definitions of a variety of social phenomena."[27] Understood from this perspective, the media become something more than just another variable in the process of social change. Mass communication and its media logic is at the heart of a collective consciousness that binds society together.[28]

Along the same lines Daniel Yankelovich suggests that there is a new convergence between social elites and mass populations in the United States. According to this view, the United States is presently undergoing a profound cultural revolution in the interplay between the economy and culture, thus giving rise to new forms of social integration.[29] If this is true, the integrating potential of mass societies is not being fully appreciated or understood.

It would be a mistake to assume that this communication process is merely a one-way series of transactions. The processes included under the term mass communication are highly interactive between communicating agents and those internalizing and acting on those messages.[30]

Richard Lipsky captures the essence of this idea in what he calls "sport-speak," a language created in order to achieve dramatic simplicity between mass communication media and an active spectatorship.[31] According to Lipsky, it is the "sportsworld which has become the arena where grace, form, and ethical content still survive." Sports not only creates a seemingly autonomous world with its own ethical imperatives (slogans, morals, legal proscriptions), it also creates a powerful communal bond,[32] and sportspeak becomes the glue that binds mass spectator audiences together. Examples abound when sports extravaganzas are televised. During the college football season, sportscaster/announcer Keith Jackson of ABC typically gives a stirring introduction, describing the tension-filled atmosphere of such epic contests as those between the "Crimson Tide" of Alabama and the "Fighting Irish" of Notre Dame. Perhaps more familiar to television audiences are the dramatic and emotionally charged opening words to ABC's highly acclaimed "Wide World of Sports." Expressions like "the thrill of victory and the agony of defeat" have become a part of the national vocabulary connecting the spectator to the events of the screen.

Walter Kerr, the retired movie critic of *The New York Times* emphasized the importance of words in television productions when he suggested that television is *not* really a visual medium, at least in the sense that movies are. He went on to suggest that TV is essentially a talk medium.[33] This idea bears further analysis. Perhaps that is why television seems to cry out for words, any kind of words, and why some people prefer to listen to their radios while watching games. It may also explain why the prodigious play diagrams of former Raider coach John Madden seem to be so appreciated. Words add dimension and texture to what is otherwise a directors' medium, with its stop frame action and instant replays.

The sports world—a simple world of competition, character, success, and defeat—is in some ways an anachronism, given the everyday realities and complexities of life in a mass bureaucratic society. This world seems remarkably well preserved, however, in the imaginations of the millions of spectators who ritualistically engage the enemy on sports weekends. This connection between televised sports presentations and a mass spectator audience would be inconceivable without the linking properties of a warm, vital, personal, and concrete sports language. Language is the essence of a culture. As sports continues to gain a greater foothold in the American imagination, its "language" permeates society; a new convergence in the psychoculture of the United States may actually be taking place. The passivity of the sports spectator has been taken for granted, but in fact there seems to be a persistent "need to believe that sport represents something more than entertainment, something that, though neither life nor death in itself, retains some of the lingering capacity to dramatize and clarify those experiences."[34]

There are, of course, other implications to be drawn from this powerful relationship between sports and culture. As entertainment becomes synonymous with the mass media, and as a language suitable for simplifying and communicating images develops, one should expect a progressive decline in the abilities of large masses of Americans to universalize beyond the limits of languages such as sportspeak. The structure or syntax of the information communicated carries with it the ability to create affecting images. This structure also educates mass audiences on how to respond to what is communicated.

By contrast, habitual television viewers attending a live event often experience some consternation and almost always a degree of disorientation at what seems to them to be sensory bombardment. At a live football, basketball, or baseball game, there is no one way to contour and select what one sees. One is confronted with a startling array of activity both on the field and off. Some even find what goes on in the stands to be more interesting than the game taking place on the field. Michael Novak has stated that sports by their very nature constitute nothing less than religion and is equally outspoken about the effects of television on sports.[35] While televised sports has given millions of spectators many hours of viewing pleasure, it has also taught how to view games. Television has in Novak's words "rendered the unaided eye weak and undisciplined." Without belaboring the point, TV misses the sense of the whole game, its intricacies, its developmental character, its very essence, and instead brings us a pinched vision of the game, focusing as it does on the so-called skilled positions. The term also defines what the camera cannot do, that is, focus on the totality of play.[36] The point here is that what takes place on television is very different from what the live presentation is all about. By its very nature, televised sports presents a set of images selected to convey the emotional and connective properties of sports, with a specialized language developed to heighten and simplify these presentations. What is presented as sports may provide a picture of life in its dramatic moments, but one is not likely to find the "beef" in such presentations.

In some ways Peter Wood comes closest to plumbing the depths of the audience's attraction to television. Wood draws an analogy between the images of television and those of dreams: both are highly symbolic, have high visual quality, and a high degree of wish fulfillment; both appear to contain much that is disjointed and trivial, have enormous and powerful content, most of which is readily and thoroughly forgotten, and both make consistent use (overt and disguised) of materials drawn from recent experiences.[37] It is possible, he ventures, that we in the audience are in some way responsible for television; not in a practical and individual way, but as a vivid projection of our own collective unconscious.

To some, television contains qualities representative of an increasingly homogenous society. To others, television foretells a future electronic community as technical developments extend television's capabilities. With greater numbers of channels, increasing audience divisibility, more display alternatives and feedback mechanisms, together with greater storage capacities for programmer and viewer, television has the potential to launch a visual communications revolution to describe the limits of which would challenge the most fertile imagination. Television's cumulative effects on society are simply not known, at least not with any degree of clarity. We seek to draw the reader's attention less to the magic of technical mechanisms than to the power of television to create and structure new consumer markets.

## Medium, Sports, and Audiences

In recent years, television networks have allocated more time to sports programming, with the result of increasing competition among national television networks and the newly emergent cable networks. Cable networks like Entertainment, Sports Programming Network, and ESPN have led the way in developing more specialized programs covering a broad range of sports programs. It is estimated, for example, that 44 percent of all sports events in 1984 was on "pay" TV and that regional pay services like Anheuser-Busch sports will carry an increasing amount of sports television. The assumption guiding these new market ventures is that spectator interest is highest in the televising of the games of local teams. The "bottom line," of course, is where networks and spectators converge in spending money.[38]

As television shapes its audiences, it develops its own logic and expectations. In the case of a major sports event—the Super Bowl, the World Series, the finals at Wimbledon, or a championship fight—television encourages the viewer to anticipate the impending contest, building excitement through advertising, for as we all know, nothing draws a crowd like a good fight. Television thus stimulates the viewer's conscious and unconscious mind in such a way that a relationship between electronic images and the viewer's own primordial memories is created, making it very easy for sports events to penetrate the psyche of many viewers.

In previous sections we examined some contemporary characteristics of television: the growth of cable networks, the specialized programming of sports events, and the flow of images and symbols from sports events to viewers. These characteristics enhance television's power to create new symbols capable of stirring the deepest projections and imaginative images of the viewer and thereby create a context for the relationship between the media and the social system. Similarly, the existence of these relationships implies a special system of power.

Sports also reinforce the social value of teamwork and in this context define the nature and benefits of individual effort. One set of values inherent in sports emphasize (where appropriate) the importance of teamwork, sometimes at the expense of individual achievement. The sports ethos, like that of the business world, stresses winning and the positive consequences of teamwork. Sports often encourage a cooperative ethos and confirm the idea that hard work produces positive rewards; violation of the cooperative ethos undermines the objectives of winning. In other words, sports in mass industrial society not only allows for the expression of competitive urges inherent in society, but also helps to discipline that expression.[39]

## Television and the Demise of the Athlete as Hero

Attention is paid to the idea of athletes as modern day heroes and to athletes' reputed effects upon the nation's impressionable youth, yet many of us have the nagging feeling that something profound has changed in the way we regard those who have achieved in athletics. Heroes just don't seem to have that "specialness" that heroes had in the past. If this is true, then what caused the change and what are the implications in light of our argument regarding television's role as the real producer of college sports?

Clearly, the world has changed greatly in the last few decades, and the notion of the hero has changed with it. In the ancient world, heroes were celebrated in myths through an entire age or epoch, but in the modern world, the hero in the classical sense has passed from the scene. The contemporary hero is a well-known person, the celebrated creation of a media production. Daniel Boorstin has suggested that democratic beliefs and new scientific insights into human behavior have nibbled away at the glamour of heroes from the past and consequently affect our ability to create heroes in the contemporary world.[40] Likewise, inherent in the notion of self-governance is the passion for equality to be shared among all citizens, accompanied by a suspicion almost bordering on distrust of heroic greatness.

What's more, the beleaguered citizen of a mass society must confront a constant assault of stimuli from a variety of media sources, including newspapers, magazines, second-class mail, books, radio, television (and its spinoff, videodiscs), and whatever the corporate technostructure will provide in the future. The very idea of the hero in such circumstances becomes less significant and necessary. The hero, then, like a spontaneous event, has become lost in the congested traffic of pseudoevents, those approximations of reality created by and for the media.[41]

Drawing upon Daniel Boorstin's cogent insights, Barbara Goldsmith further asserts that ours has become an age in which, by contrast with the "real thing," "the synthetic product has become so seductive and malleable that we no longer care to distinguish one from another."[42] Confusion develops in the public mind when old values and traditional norms are applied to those who are adulated in the mass media. The substitution of image in our high-tech world for the mundane reality of daily living explains the growth and attractiveness of the sports hero as sports celebrity, and this trend is not likely to diminish in the future. In fact, this system is so productive that it can more than match the public's ability to absorb pseudoevents and synthetic personalities.

For example, who can fail to notice that some star athletes and sports celebrities seem to have become the center almost of cults, which in themselves are shared experiences for the participants. Fans will often crowd around their favorite players, hoping perhaps to retrieve some talisman or just to be in the presence of that special "gift of grace"? At an airport recently, while waiting for the usual congestion to subside prior to boarding, this author noticed a small but agitated group of people surrounding someone later discovered to be Lynn Swann, the former All-Pro flanker for the Pittsburgh Steelers. Particularly striking was not so much the picture of autograph hunters seeking legible scribble on a piece of paper, but the intensity of the interaction, especially in the case of the surrounding men. Both men and women presented Swann with pen and paper, but more important, they seemed to seek something more mysterious from the manner in which they tried to "touch" him. He had what social theorists call *charisma,* a gift of grace, and those who crowded around him almost reverently wanted to partake of it. Lynn Swann had retired by this time from active play with the Pittsburgh Steelers, but he nevertheless retained that specialness, that mysterious alchemy of stardom. It is no wonder that he continues his career as a sports celebrity/color commentator for one of the networks.

While the acrobatic Lynn Swann retains his gift of grace, the man of the hour in 1984 has to be the little big-man from Boston College, Doug Flutie. No one in recent years has been the object of so much media attention and hype as has this gifted quarterback, who in addition to leading his team to three successive bowl victories, has single-handedly set little Boston College on a par with Notre Dame, USC, Nebraska, and Michigan.

Flutie's meteoric rise and importance cannot be assessed adequately by a mere recitation of his athletic achievements, but doing so will help to establish the basis for his prominence. As was reported in the *Los Angeles Times,* Flutie set two NCAA career records: 10,579 yards by passing and 11,054 yards in total offense. He won the Heisman Trophy without any serious opposition and became the first white player to win it since Archie Griffin in 1973 began the winning streak of black running backs; this fact adds immeasurably to both his personal and market acceptability. As if this were not enough, he was a candidate for a Rhodes scholarship, threw a touchdown pass to his brother during the final game of the season, and gave his high school sweetheart an engagement ring for Christmas. How can someone miss with timing like this?[43]

Doug Flutie has brought money to television stations and to Boston College as a result of his attractive media presence based on unparalleled athletic achievements, but his magic extends even further into the marketplace. In Boston an ice cream flavor is named after him: "Tutti Flutie." The *Los Angeles Times* reported that more than four-hundred-thousand dollars' worth of Eagle (the name of Boston College's athletic team) souvenirs were sold by the Boston College bookstores before Christmas and that the bookstores expected to sell another one-hundred-thousand dollars' worth of Flutie memorabilia.[44] These figures represent record sales according to the major supplier of such items to college bookstores. Flutie alone beat out the reigning champion merchandiser, North Carolina State, which had won the 1983 NCAA basketball tournament. As one might suspect, items bearing number twenty-two were by far the best sellers.

To say that Doug Flutie has become a media event is to draw attention to the obvious. To suggest further that he is money in the bank for television producers and for Boston College is clear and reveals the organizational power of the sports business system and its ability to generate revenue around a star performer. Doug Flutie has gone beyond the normal descriptions of greatness and athletic brilliance; he has charisma. His achievements are described as being more than ordinarily brilliant, for he creates miracles like his Hail Mary pass in the final seconds of a game, defeating the University of Miami and its exceptional quarterback Bernie Kosar. This 5-feet-9-and-¾-inch (he insists on adding the ¾ of an inch to his height) multitalented football player is considered an authentic American Hero, embodying as he does the hopes and dreams of millions, at least so the media tells us. The last word on this subject goes to Gill Brandt, the Dallas Cowboys' vice president, who must have sensed even greater marketing opportunities for Flutie when he said, "People in America are starved for heroes, and he's a hero."[45]

Richard Lipsky believes that this kind of "heroism" helps solve the problem of individual alienation by relating the impersonal bureaucratic structure of our technological society to the drama of individual accomplishment.[46] By this analysis, Flutie and others are perhaps more important to the cohesion of American society than some might think.

The point is a good one, but it only begins to describe the meaning and importance of the "star performer" in a society whose sporting scene is pervaded by market values.[47] Although special distinction has always been awarded to famous performers in the arts, theater, and athletics, the "star system" (a system that includes huge profits for the famous few) is probably more important in modern capitalistic society than in times past. Responsible for this change is the growth and power of mass media to create and structure mass markets. Michael Jackson's phenomenal market appeal through records, videodiscs, books, live concerts, and television represents just one extraordinary use of the star system to increase the capacity of commodity producers.

The star system also allows for the transference of "charisma" to other commodities "sold" to a mass public. For example, Michael Jackson recently attracted one of the largest groups of "news" and television reporters when he linked his name (and "grace") with that of the president of the United States as part of a campaign to fight the use of drugs among the nation's young people. This act of heroic largess prompted Johnny Carson to remark on television that President Reagan ought to be applauded for inviting to the White House the only person who could beat him in the upcoming presidential election. Obviously, this was only a joke but Michael Jackson's popularity, as fostered by the media, is very real.

The basic principle of the star system is that there is a direct relationship between the exceptional performer and audience appeal, and that appeal, of course, means profits. When it comes to television production of sports programming, the star system not only applies to individual stars, but to teams as well.[48]

Another important element in the star system is television's ability to meet the needs of a public overwhelmed by the rapid advance of technology. The alienation of people from technology is not new, but what does seem new about the public's relationship to technology is people's growing dependence on information filtered through that technology, with the result that the world of the pseudoevent (as presented by television) is becoming increasingly the world of the general public. We have discovered a circular relationship between the productive forces in society and the projected needs, wishes, and aspirations of the great mass of the population. Is it any wonder then that television, movie, music, and sports celebrities rank at the top of the lists of people Americans most recognize and admire?

Success in sports is at one level a product of an exceptional blending of individual and team effort, and yet at the same time the unique contribution of the star (or media hero) is recognized as a significant, even essential ingredient in securing great victories for the team, to say nothing of profits for the owners. Through the vehicle of television, the actions of the exceptional athlete can be dramatically captured in a unique moment of uniquely high performance. In this way, television magnifies such performances, making them seem to be immediate experiences for the mass audience, and documenting the exceptional talent of the sports hero, whose physical performance cannot easily be replicated by ordinary athletes.

That sports is one of the few domains in which heroes come to life partly accounts for the extraordinary power of sports in the American imagination. In televised sports such values as competition, power, aggressiveness, and teamwork are communicated to millions. Sports is also associated with physical discipline, and the persistence of a strong work ethic is implied in both college and professional sports performance. Actions explicitly confirming that sports is an entertainment business evoke public resistance. For this reason, perhaps, the public resents the extension of labor disputes and other "real world" aspects into professional sports. On the other hand, the public applauds exceptional individual sports performance because of the intense mythic images associated with sports. In sports, as in most things, tension exists between myth and reality; television seems to make it more difficult for people to discern the difference.

Finally, we must examine the extent to which television changes the sports hero and the implications of this change for intercollegiate athletics. After all is said and done, one effect of television on fame and obscurity seems clear: television exhausts obscurity. It makes the unfamiliar familiar and in the process elevates the much-discussed media personality to the point where he is essential to the marketing of sports.

This relationship between television and sports implies some costs to the notion of the student-athlete as hero. We accept as conventional wisdom that commercialism has permeated intercollegiate sports, and one effect of commercialism is that the college athlete has become symbolically tainted. No longer is the college athlete, especially the star performer, simply viewed as the big man on campus. Increasingly, the athlete's presence is appreciated as necessary for the production and elevation of sports at the university. In other words, the star performer's value to his university is in his exceptional athletic talent and the economic worth of that talent in drawing large audiences. The publicity given to athletes like John Elway of Stanford University, Herschel Walker, formerly of the University of Georgia, the troubled Marcus Dupree, and Doug Flutie illustrates the length to which universities and colleges will go to promote the exceptional performer on whose shoulder pads rest the fortunes of the institution's athletic future.

## Reflections on the Role of the Media in Mass Society

Most people have negative associations with the term *mass society.* The term is commonly associated with the creation of low-level sensations and standardized products.[49] Some critics have pointed out that the creation of postindustrial mass societies implies a degree of rootlessness, alienation, moral emptiness, conformism, belieflessness, atomization, homogeneity, and facelessness,[50] and while we agree with this analysis to a certain extent, we think these converging "characteristics" of mass society are exaggerated. Focusing on the presumed pathological aspects of mass societies can cause one to overlook new, critical variables associated with new forms of corporatism.

One such element in American society is a new kind of dualism. The workplace requires a more communitarian ethos, and at the same time, the individual becomes more open to new personal experiences and creative impulses. We are witnessing the simultaneous "individuation" of people's lives and the diminution of cultural variations, including those of class and profession.[51]

We think that conventional assumptions about mass society tend to ignore the different creative syntheses likely to occur in a more fluid society; an overly negative appraisal of the mass media undoubtedly contributes to this perspective. The interwoven and often unintentional effects of the media in mass society are little understood by elites and masses alike, but in any case, the mass media now have enormous power: they influence the decisions and actions of public officials; they insulate powerful interests that have the most to say about the use of the media; they reallocate power among the already powerful; they blunt and filter the ability of the people to judge and to act quickly in what may be their self-interest; they foment discontent among people; and last, they preserve the legitimacy of the political, economic, and social status quo.

Mass societies have the power to establish new corporate structures around which mass culture can assume new and unanticipated forms. Within this context we can more clearly understand how and why corporation-owned television, driven by the imperatives to create new markets, develops and refines the form of its particular commodity, at the same time presenting this form as the essence of modern sports.[52]

Sports in mass society functions as a culturally integrating symbol: that sports is presented as a social event on television makes it a life-giving symbol. Since traditional cultural symbols associated with family, birth, death, and marriage seem to have lost much of their content, sports has become a more distinctive symbol of mass culture in advanced industrial societies like that of the United States.

As cultures have done in earlier periods, contemporary society presents a refurbished set of symbols. In sports, we see this process reconstituting old-fashioned American values (competition, conflict, teamwork, individual effort) in a new socioeconomic context. For example, sports celebrities in recent years have advanced the commercialization of athletics through their advertisements for special products. In this way prominent, professional athletes expand a sports infrastructure because by endorsing a particular product the well-known athlete infuses novel commercial content into television, and although data on such processes are not available, we can assume that similar commercial exchanges exist within intercollegiate sports—a process that reinforces latent commercialization.

Clearly, television plays a major role in extending the structure of corporate athleticism. It is the mechanism for marketing most of the highly developed sports products. Further, television advertisements extend the domain of athleticism in several other ways. The movement of football players into professional sports in the junior year of college is another illustration of the way television accelerates the professionalization of intercollegiate sports. That is to say, the market value of a given college athlete is partly a function of the way sports commentators focus attention on that individual's exceptional (quasi-professional) skills. The marketability of college athletes is also affected by the way the intercollegiate sports infrastructure in many respects parallels the organizational structures of professional sports; this parallelism facilitates the early movement of college stars into the professional ranks.

Television is also affecting college athletics by creating new markets for sports programming. Cable television, via subnational and subregional markets, is creating a more differentiated market structure. As a result, professional sports recruiters are increasingly able to identify sports talent in secondary markets—at small, non-Division I and less prestigious schools.

Television, in sum, does not simply present sports. It also translates sports activities into the market medium. What constitutes sports is what television markets to mass audiences as sports. Through its own mechanisms, it influences the popular definition of any sport. In a sense, it also produces the perceptions that define sports standards. Because it organizes large-scale markets, television creates the sports superstar. Television, not universities, is ultimately the producer of college sports.

In addition to presenting social values, television performs other valuable functions. It possesses the technological ability to shape the broad evolution of corporate athleticism: it can reach national audiences, segment regional markets, and organize specialized sports stations. By reaching contractual agreements with universities and the NCAA to televise the best teams, it promotes top-rank college sports standards. Because television frequently broadcasts games between traditional rivals, it can sustain regional markets. Indeed, the cumulative effects of each sports season—now increasingly defined according to television markets rather than traditional sports seasons—are presented on television in the different NCAA bowl appearances and national basketball championships. By moving college sports away from the campus, television connects sports to its wider sports clientele.

Since World War II there has been both a qualitative and quantitative change in how Americans use leisure time. On the one hand, people have more time available for leisure activities; on the other, more people are spending that time "watching" television as opposed to engaging in other kinds of activities. Sports, as we have noted, is prominently showcased as one of the most popular forms of mass entertainment. As an entertainment medium, television restructures social categories in such a way that people can respond to televised sports in nonclass-specific terms. You can be either for or against, say, the Dallas Cowboys; it doesn't matter whether you practice law or sweep floors for a living. This is one example of television's astounding ability to reshape mass spectator audiences through sports events.

Another example can be seen in television's transformation of what in the past would have been a parochial contest between two teams into a package appealing to a national audience. For example, a traditional contest between regional football rivals like UCLA and USC can be sold and packaged on television as a contest with national appeal. The networks use the same strategy in marketing other kinds of sports events, too. The peak event or contest is presented to the national audience *regardless* of which particular sport is involved—a tennis match between McEnroe and Lendl, the Kentucky Derby, the New York marathon; the list goes on.

By combining technical virtuosity in dramatic presentation with high-level competition and a focus on the superstar performers, television has become the prime medium for calling up the primordial sentiments of sports fans. "Sportspeak" evokes sentiment and drama that connect "televiewing" man with "telematic" images; sports simply would not be the same without Howard Cosell "Telling It Like It Is" or Keith Jackson elevating a pushing and shoving match between undergraduate men to the height of Greek drama. The social factor of increased leisure time combined with the technical and economic factors of corporate-owned broadcast television have created a new sports market. All of these conditions, working together, enhance the production of sports as a commercial product.

## Notes

1. David Marc, "Understanding Television," *The Atlantic Monthly* (August 1984):33.

2. John P. Robinson and Philip E. Converse, "Social Change Reflected in the Use of Time," in *The Human Meaning of Social Change,* ed. Angus Campbell and Philip E. Converse (New York: Russell Sage Foundation, 1972), 17–86.

3. Ibid., 29.

4. Ibid., 37.

5. Ibid., 40–41.

6. The Miller Lite Report (Milwaukee, Wis.: Miller Brewing Co., 1983).

7. Ibid., 17.

8. Ibid., 18.

9. Ibid., 18–20.

10. Robert D. Kahn, "More Messages from the Medium," *Technology Review* 86, no. 1 (January 1983):49–51.

11. James Martin, *The Telematic Society* (Englewood Cliffs, N.J.: Prentice-Hall, Inc., 1981), 34.

12. Kahn, "More Messages," 49.

13. Ibid.

14. Ibid.

15. Ibid., 50.

16. Ibid.

17. Jerry Mander, *Four Arguments for the Elimination of Television* (New York: Quill, 1978), 126.

18. Peter W. Bernstein, "The Race to Feed Cable TV's Maw," *Fortune* 103, no. 9 (May 4, 1981):308–18.

19. Michael Emery and Ted Curtis Smythe, *Readings in Mass Communication,* 5th ed. (Dubuque, Iowa: William C. Brown Co., 1983), 249.

20. Bernstein, "The Race to Feed Cable TV's Maw," 345.

21. Martin L. Ernst, "Cable's Economic Impacts," *Technology Review* 86, no. 1 (January 1983), 52–55.

22. Ralph Nader, "Access in the Eighties," in Emery, and Smythe, *Readings in Mass Communication,* 135–41.

23. Michael Novak, *The Joy of Sports* (New York: Basic Books, 1976), 12.

24. Entman and Paletz, 171.

25. Novak, *The Joy of Sports,* 50.

26. Mander, *Four Arguments,* 113–33.

27. David L. Altheide and Robert P. Snow, *Media Logic* (Beverly Hills, Calif.: Sage Publications, 1979), 237, 59.

28. Altheide and Snow, *Media Logic,* 237.

29. Daniel Yankelovich, *New Rules: Searching for Self-Fulfillment in a World Turned Upside Down* (Toronto: Bantam Books, 1981), 157–58.

30. Altheide and Snow, *Media Logic,* 10.

31. Richard Lipsky, *How We Play the Game* (Boston: Beacon Press, 1981), 136–38.

32. Ibid., 136.

33. Walter Kerr, "In Praising Silence in Film," *New York Times Magazine,* 30 (September 1984), 42–46, 50–55.

34. Christopher Lasch, *The Culture of Narcissism,* (New York: Norton-Simon, 1979), 119.

35. Novak, *Joy of Sports,* 254.

36. Ibid., 250.

37. Peter H. Wood, "Television as a Dream, in *Television as a Cultural Force,* ed. Richard Adler and Douglass Cater (New York: Praeger Publishers, 1976), 17–35.

38. *Sports Illustrated,* 2 April 1984, 78.

39. Lasch, *The Culture of Narcissism,* 116.

40. Daniel Boorstin, *The Image* (New York: Athenaeum, 1977), 49.

41. Ibid., 53.

42. Barbara Goldsmith, *New York Times Magazine,* 4 December 1983, 75.

43. *Los Angeles Times,* 30 December 1984, 14.

44. Ibid.

45. Ibid.

46. Richard Lipsky, *How We Play the Game,* 213.

47. Lasch, *The Culture of Narcissism,* 117.

48. Richard Sennet, *The Fall of Public Man* (New York: Vintage Books, 1974), 287–93.

49. Muriel G. Cantor, *Prime Time Television: Content and Control* (Beverly Hills, Calif.: Sage Publications, 1980), 103–10.

50. Edward Shils, *Center and Periphery: Essays in Macro-Sociology* (Chicago: University of Chicago Press, 1975), 91–107.

51. Ibid. 101.

52. Richard Grunneau, *Class, Sports, and Social Development* (Amherst, Mass.: University of Massachusetts Press, 1983), 123.

# 5
# The Economic Base of Corporate Athleticism

The rise of television and the expansion of sports commercialism have made athletics extremely profitable for some universities, and this chapter focuses attention on the market dimensions of the corporate athletic structure. Our subject here is mainly those universities and colleges that have attained national reputations as sports powers—such schools as Notre Dame, USC, the Universities of Alabama and Oklahoma, along with twenty-five or so other universities and colleges whose names have become synonymous with big-time college athletics;[1] these are the schools commonly termed the "money machines" of college athletics. The imperatives to become more businesslike and to develop "more promotions, more effective marketing strategies, and more shares of the institutional assets sold to donors, television, the holder of needed resources to fund uncontrolled growth" seems to be the lot of most of the semiprofessional college sports programs.[2] Universities and colleges engaged in these programs can be categorized in various ways, but for our purposes, we will describe institutions engaged in athletics according to the ways in which their programs are financed.

Atwell et al. have ferreted out the overlapping and confusing elements involved in financing college sports.[3] We have borrowed heavily from their classification system and would add only, as they do, that no classification scheme can include all the differences that may exist among the many athletic programs under the regulatory control of several intercollegiate governing bodies.

We submit, however, that the concept of corporate athleticism, while immediately applicable to the easily recognized "big powers" in collegiate athletics, may also be applied to any sports program that manages its sports program in such a way as to achieve maximum financial return. In these times of financial retrenchment and rising educational costs, few institutions would not fall into this category. Any university or college regardless of size, ethnic or racial make-up, and academic standing, can take on the values of corporate athleticism. We speak of these values in terms of degree, but matters of degree can easily involve qualitative differences as well.

## The Semiprofessional Model

While university and college athletic programs may be seen as comprising several models, our focus is on the semiprofessional, intercollegiate model— distinguished usually by the largest and most commercialized athletic programs. The universities to be most closely examined are the so-called money machines alluded to earlier. The semiprofessional designation fits the "major" sports of football and basketball and may not fully apply to the "minor" sports like field hockey, volleyball, track and field, and swimming. Although this analysis is applied largely to football and basketball, many of the generalizations offered are also valid, in varying degrees, with respect to trends in the so-called minor sports.

*Revenue Sources*

One might assume that all programs considered to be semiprofessional are money-making programs, but this is far from the truth. Only a small number of football programs are classified as Division I-A, and within this grouping schools that make up the College Football Association (CFA) are significantly "richer" in terms of both gate receipts and television revenues than the others. Many college and university athletic programs seldom earn a profit, instead they cost money, even though approximately $700 million in revenue was generated from all college sports in 1981. Approximately 2 percent of all schools and 40 percent of the so-called major athletic powers finished in the red.[4] Don Canham, the University of Michigan's "promotion-minded" athletic director, estimated that his is one of the twenty or twenty-five schools in the country whose sports programs pay their own way.[5] The trend of the fat cats of collegiate athletics getting fatter was noted by the NCAA in 1977, and it continues and will probably continue in the future.[6]

In most cases, institutions following the semiprofessional model have developed administrative structures "separated" from the traditional academic organization of the university.[7] Suffice it to say here that the "semi-autonomous" character of administrative relations between the sports complex and the central administration gives athletic directors easy and special access to educational administrators directly responsible for the financial futures of the athletic departments; and, needless to say, it allows for coordination and planning of presidential strategies and athletic department interests.

There has been a dramatic change in the lineup of the big powers in the last twenty to twenty-five years. In the past, prominent private universities and colleges held sway in the public's imagination of football Saturday. Now, mainly because of escalating costs, the major contestants for national intercollegiate honors are primarily state institutions. Unlike private institutions, many public institutions are able to have a large part of their grant-in-aid and scholarship budgets subsidized.[8]

According to a recent NCAA study, seven major revenue sources generate a substantial percentage of the total revenues of most Division I, Class A universities and colleges.[9] These institutions must play more than 50 percent of their regular football games against other Division I members in that sport; sports other than football must be classified as Division I, also according to NCAA rules. The sources of revenue include:

1. Total ticket sales to the public, students, and university staff, not reduced by guarantees subsequently paid;
2. Student activity fees covering admissions, not included in (1);
3. Student activity fees or assessments not related to athletic admissions;
4. Guarantees and options received;
5. Contributions from alumni and others;
6. Distributions from conference or other associations from bowl games, tournaments, or television;
7. Direct state or other government support.[10]

Table 5–1 summarizes these seven revenue sources for fiscal 1981 and illustrates the significance of these categories of revenue production. The teams of Class A institutions compose the most attractive entertainment events for on-site attendance and for television viewing. These institutions depend heavily on ticket sales and game contract settlements. Other institutions rely more heavily on student activity fees and assessments. The reasons make it clear why so many universities seem willing to refurbish old stadiums, or as at West Virginia University, to build new ones capable of seating more fans. As we shall see, stadium size and removal from old, congested campuses is one indicator of a university's commitment to corporate athleticism in its athletic program.

Controlling the overall costs of sports entertainment remains a persistent problem at universities and colleges. Furthermore, several NCAA studies indicate a marked increase in both total revenues and expenses between 1977 and 1981; notably, expenses in most divisions exceed revenues, with the exception of Class A programs.[11] It seems, from the data displayed in table 5–2, that if present trends continue (and there is little reason to think that they won't) many athletic programs will sooner or later be in financial difficulty.

The pressures generated by a public eager to identify with a winning athletic program and those created by the media compound the basic problems of controlling athletic programs' finances, and these pressures are

# Table 5–1
## Analysis of Principal Revenue Sources: Fiscal Year 1981
*(dollar amounts in thousands)*

| Revenue Source | Class A | Class B | Class C | Class D | Class E | Class F |
|---|---|---|---|---|---|---|
| Total ticket sales not reduced by contract settlements | $1,489 | $ 64 | $ 20 | $177 | $ 18 | $ 3 |
| Percentage of total | 43% | 23% | 28% | 34% | 14% | 2% |
| Student activity fees for athletic admissions | $ 393 | $176 | $103 | $164 | $ 89 | $59 |
| Percentage of total | 6% | 20% | 12% | 17% | 9% | 13% |
| Student assessments unrelated to admissions | $ 301 | $172 | $104 | $238 | $146 | $98 |
| Percentage of total | 2% | 17% | 26% | 10% | 32% | 56% |
| Guarantees and options received | $ 363 | $ 20 | $ 11 | $ 25 | $ 6 | $ 2 |
| Percentage of total | 10% | 5% | 5% | 4% | 3% | 1% |
| Contributions from alumni and others | $ 437 | $ 31 | $ 16 | $ 96 | $ 27 | $ 9 |
| Percentage of total | 11% | 4% | 7% | 14% | 12% | 4% |
| Distribution from conferences and other associations | $ 368 | $ 16 | $ 25 | $ 52 | $ 4 | $10 |
| Percentage of total | 10% | 2% | 9% | 5% | 1% | 2% |
| Direct state or other governmental support | $ 514 | $176 | $ 48 | $262 | $159 | $81 |
| Percentage of total | 6% | 25% | 2% | 5% | 26% | 14% |
| All other revenues | $ 517 | $ 23 | $ 31 | $ 99 | $ 12 | $17 |
| Percentage of total | 12% | 4% | 11% | 11% | 3% | 8% |

Source: Mitchell H. Raiborn, "Revenues and Expenses of Intercollegiate Athletic Programs—Analysis of Financial Trends and Relationships, 1978–81."

Table 5-2
Comparative Averages for Total Revenues and Expenses: Fiscal Years 1974–1981
(dollar amounts in thousands)

| Respondent Category | 1974 | 1975 | 1976 | 1977 | 1978 | 1979 | 1980 | 1981 |
|---|---|---|---|---|---|---|---|---|
| **Class A Institutions** | | | | | | | | |
| Total revenues | $1,708 | $1,849 | $2,085 | $2,183 | $2,368 | $2,581 | $2,959 | $3,391 |
| Total expenses | 1,781 | 1,924 | 2,096 | 2,213 | 2,238 | 2,360 | 2,875 | 3,243 |
| Implied (deficit) or profit[a] | (73) | (75) | (11) | (30) | 130 | 121 | 84 | 148 |
| **Class B Institutions** | | | | | | | | |
| Total revenues | $ 229 | $ 236 | $ 276 | $ 311 | $ 164 | $ 182 | $ 212 | $ 248 |
| Total expenses | 369 | 392 | 412 | 460 | 287 | 322 | 355 | 392 |
| Implied deficit | (140) | (156) | (136) | (149) | (123) | (140) | (143) | (144) |
| **Class C Institutions** | | | | | | | | |
| Total revenues | $ 47 | $ 50 | $ 53 | $ 55 | $ 40 | $ 45 | $ 51 | $ 56 |
| Total expenses | 145 | 153 | 162 | 171 | 188 | 201 | 221 | 249 |
| Implied deficit | (98) | (103) | (109) | (116) | (148) | (156) | (170) | (193) |
| **Class D Institutions** | | | | | | | | |
| Total revenues | $ 135 | $ 133 | $ 163 | $ 196 | $ 277 | $ 343 | $ 384 | $ 476 |
| Total expenses | 252 | 255 | 289 | 317 | 410 | 476 | 563 | 631 |
| Implied deficit | (117) | (122) | (126) | (121) | (133) | (133) | (179) | (155) |
| **Class E Institutions** | | | | | | | | |
| Total revenues | $ 64 | $ 87 | $ 163 | $ 69 | $ 74 | $ 77 | $ 86 | $ 102 |
| Total expenses | 137 | 157 | 135 | 146 | 163 | 166 | 180 | 232 |
| Implied (deficit) or profit | (73) | (70) | 28 | (77) | (89) | (89) | (94) | (130) |
| **Class F Institutions** | | | | | | | | |
| Total revenues | $ 38 | $ 37 | $ 37 | $ 39 | $ 24 | $ 26 | $ 29 | $ 30 |
| Total expenses | 67 | 72 | 76 | 83 | 106 | 121 | 129 | 144 |
| Implied deficit | (29) | (35) | (39) | (44) | (82) | (95) | (100) | (114) |

Source: Mitchell H. Raiborn

[a]Deficit is used to decrease an excess of expenses over revenues.
Profit is used to decrease an excess of revenues over expenses.

**Table 5–3**
**Revenue Sources as a Percentage of Total Revenues: Fiscal Years**
**1973, 1977, and 1981**

| | Class A Group | | |
|---|---|---|---|
| *Revenue Sources* | *1973* | *1977* | *1981* |
| Total ticket sales | 48% | 47% | 43% |
| Student activity fees | 8 | 7 | 6 |
| Student assessments | 3 | 12 | 10 |
| Guarantees and options | 12 | 12 | 10 |
| Contributions from alumni | 7 | 10 | 11 |
| Distributions—Special Events | 10 | 10 | 10 |
| Government support | 2 | 2 | 6 |
| All other revenues | 10 | 10 | 12 |

Source: Mitchell H. Raiborn

unlikely to diminish in the near future. Although the principal revenue sources should remain fairly constant in value, they have apparently decreased since 1973 as a percentage of total revenues (table 5–3).[12]

If the existing athletic programs are to survive, lost revenues must be replaced. These revenues seem to be coming from "unearned and passive" sources, that is, student assessments, contributions, and government, the latter being an important source of revenue for public institutions. The significance of this pattern must not be lost. As costs increase relative to revenue-generating capacity and as the main sources of revenue decrease as a percentage of total revenues, athletic programs will have to rely increasingly on outside contributions for support. For this reason, the role of alumni and boosters has become so important.

According to one analyst, donations make up the fastest rising source of income for big-school athletic programs. In 1969, contributions amounted to 5 percent of athletic budgets; in 1981 they jumped to 11 percent. Further underscoring the importance of gifts, this same analyst stated: "Pull the gifts and relatively few schools would break even on sports. That's how expensive—and competitive—they've become."[13]

## Control of Intercollegiate Athletics

Universities and colleges do not seem to be totally in control of intercollegiate athletics. This provokes the question, who is? To a large extent, universities have bestowed control of athletics on alumni and other supporters who provide resources, and this cluster of interests has assumed informal control of big-time intercollegiate athletics. While we agree that individual institutions can do little to control the costs of athletic programs and that "athletic governing bodies have not acted in any significant ways to control costs,"[14] we do not agree that the power to control such costs lies exclusively with the NCAA or with any other "regulatory" agency.

The imperatives for college sports to operate according to business principles and to develop "more promotions, more effective marketing strategies, and more shares of the institutional assets sold to donors, television, and the holder of needed resources to fund uncontrolled growth" seems to be the lot of most semiprofessional programs.[15] The solution, according to one observer, is not to eliminate semiprofessional athletics, as the University of San Francisco did in basketball for a brief time, but to control the programs so that they fit educational institutions without driving them to bankruptcy.[16]

This solution sounds good, but it is based on certain assumptions about what constitutes the problem. We here part company with those who posit that dependence on gate receipts and external funding sources stems from the refusal of universities with semiprofessional programs to regard sports as a valid component of the educational programs. We disagree with the argument that athletic programs should be structured and financed in a manner similar to that of academic departments.

Nothing draws a crowd like a good fight, and this principle goes a long way in explaining way the programs of so many universities and colleges, the crème de la crème of big-time athletics, are judged on the basis of their ability to attract large numbers of spectators and huge television audiences. This principle also helps to explain the continuing and rising investment in the production costs, including recruitment of top-flight athletes, expenditure on infrastructure (for example, new lights for football stadiums and training facilities), and other items considered necessary for a university to compete with other institutions for equivalent returns on investments.

That so many schools apparently want to secure these positional goods strengthens this claim. A persistent chorus is heard from athletic directors, coaches, players, boosters, students, and government officials, who want to "crack the big time," to attract national media attention via high national rankings and lucrative appearances on national or regional television. To be eligible for positional goods, universities and colleges must engage in what John Rooney has aptly termed the *recruiting game,* an activity so frustrating and dishonest that it has to be described as collegiate sports' "most miserable affliction."[17]

## The Demographics of Recruiting

Recruiting topflight athletes to fuel the nation's sports entertainment sector can be described in the worst possible moral and ethical terms, but as long as universities and colleges continue to pursue sports "excellence" on the gridiron and in the basketball arenas, they will need a substantial labor pool from which to recruit the most talented athletic performers. This pool is shrinking with the decline in the number of college-aged males, making the recruiting process more competitive than ever. Schools already rich in talent will remain at the greatest advantage in the search for prime athletic talent, because of, among other things, the unequal regional production of high-caliber players and the grossly expanded "needs" of institutions for players in sparsely populated states.[18] Production and consumption disparities help to explain why the recruitment of athletic talent is such a costly, laborious, frustrating, and sometimes dishonest necessity, and may also explain some of the many reasons for the extraordinary "cheating" that has become a central part of intercollegiate sports.[19] We hasten to add, however, that while the scarcity of talent may intensify the hunt for it, by itself such scarcity constitutes an insufficient explanation for the widespread cheating practices condemned without much effect by fans, presidents of universities and colleges, and the NCAA. We have argued that cheating can usefully be seen as a "necessary" business calculation in the quest for the winning edge, and like all business risks, the rewards for success pay handsomely in terms of gate receipts and television contracts, precisely, in other words, in the terms that matter most to semiprofessional college programs and their supporters.

The entertainment value of college sports is heightened—and especially appreciated—in those cities or states that cannot support a professional franchise. Much of the South, Southwest, and Midwest include such cities and states; West Virginia, for example, with its revitalized sports programs, illustrates this point nicely. Sandwiched between metropolitan areas in Pennsylvania and Ohio, West Virginia University has developed a serious, high-quality, high-cost sports program to serve the entertainment needs of an economically marginal state. In states in which the private sector fails to provide sports entertainment, a strong university sports tradition is likely to fill the void caused by the absence of a professional sports franchise. In small, underpopulated states, college sports may functionally substitute for market failure, so that in these situations, university presidents may find it politically impossible, given the active role of sports constituencies, to resist the rush towards corporate athleticism.

Urban concentration seems to be related to concentrated athletic talent. For example, the urbanized areas of Los Angeles and Chicago produce approximately 20 percent of all of the football players in the United States. In Texas Dallas, Fort Worth, and Houston dominate the production of athletic talent. Illinois, New York, Massachusetts, New Jersey, Florida, and Louisiana are also prime producing areas.[20]

Within this demographic context black athletes can usefully be discussed. Blacks are for the most part an urban population and not coincidentally are concentrated in locales where the search for athletic talent is most intense: high percentages of blacks on football and basketball teams come from the Detroit, Pittsburgh, Boston, to Washington, D.C., triangle. The New York metropolitan area alone produces approximately 7 percent of the country's major basketball talent, and much, if not most, of it is black. Since universities in the same area recruit much of this prime athletic talent (and probably will continue to do so), one can presume that pressures on competing institutions in other regions will continue to mount. This situation holds true for the most successful athletic producers and equally for universities that aspire to be "contenders" for positional rewards, even though they lack the population base for effective, big-time competition. These deficit areas include the Deep South, the Mid-Atlantic states, New England, the northern Midwest, and the southwestern part of the United States. There seems to be little overlap between the general distribution of population and market demand, and the market demands, make no mistake about that.

Another factor in concentrating athletic talent is the cost of maintaining programs. One result of these high costs will be the stabilization of the effective pool of rich schools, and this may already have occurred in the form of the College Football Association, which consists of the sixty-one largest and most competitive semiprofessional programs. A second result is that more competition will intensify the need to adjust existing, regulatory boundaries affecting the recruitment of athletic talent. The location of prime athletic talent suggests which schools are likely to remain in the hunt for the rewards of positional rank, with its financial payoffs of large, live spectator attendance and large, prime-time television audiences. Clearly, the rich sports powers are likely to get richer and to attempt to adjust regulatory controls to make their situation better still.

Third, while the geographic dispersion of athletic talent contributes to the pressure to break the recruiting "rules of the game," the most compelling reasons for the intensity of the recruiting game come from market forces that induce willing competitors to make breaking the recruitment rules, in effect, one of the rules of the game.[21] Schools located in nonurban, sparsely populated areas must compete actively and take higher risks to obtain the results that urbanization and population density have bestowed on the fortunate few in the metropolitan regions.

## The Underground Economy

Perhaps no financial aspect of big-time college sports is more difficult to document than the underground economy. It directly and indirectly generates a cash flow, if not profits, to the athletic departments, to the coaching staffs and assistants, and to the local businesses in and around the site of the games.

This economy comprises the many kinds of support generated by alumni, boosters, and other contributors to corporate athleticism in college sports.

Let us examine a few examples of the kinds of support granted a winning coach's program, for these examples indicate the depth of commercialization in big-time athletics. North Carolina State University's Jim Valvano experienced a sudden meteoric rise to intercollegiate basketball supremacy when his basketball team won the 1982–83 championship. Among Valvano's rewards was a deal with Hardee's fast-food chain that he would serve as speaker at the firm's management seminars, for which he reportedly received fifty thousand dollars.[22] In another case, University of Iowa Athletic Director Bump Elliot apparently has set up a private trust fund to help former coach Lute Olsen pay his children's college expenses; this fund supplements Olsen's fifty-eight-thousand-dollar-a-year base salary. Interestingly, Olsen had resigned from his position at Iowa after nine years to become head football coach at Arizona, but moving out of Iowa does not seem to have interfered with the "perks" and business arrangements he had made previously in Iowa City.[23]

The range and depth of the benefits bestowed on a successful big-time college or university coach is further illustrated by the successful suit filed by Franklin Cullen "Pepper" Rodgers, Jr., following his dismissal from the Georgia Institute of Technology. Immediately after being fired, Rodgers sued the Georgia Tech Athletic Association for the lost fringe benefits and perquisites that came along with his head football coaching position. He claimed damages for the loss of many things: his television show; a new Cadillac he received every six months; secretarial and administrative assistance; free membership and tabs at private clubs; reserved stadium booths with forty seats; paid automobile insurance premiums; free gasoline and oil; free training table meals; gifts from alumni and others; and speaking honoraria from such firms as General Motors Corporation, International Business Machines (IBM), and others. All told, he claimed damages for 1980–81 amounting to $486,980.[24] At last report, Rodgers and Georgia Tech had agreed to an out-of-court settlement; according to Tech's athletic director, an "amicable compromise" had been reached and all litigation dropped.[25] Clearly, the big-time coach is in a good position to bargain for a variety of appealing benefits, many of which are supplied by the underground economy.

Boosters also play a significant part in the underground economy. As was indicated earlier, athletic programs, especially those described here as semiprofessional, rely increasingly on outside contributions in their quest for revenue, and as a consequence, representatives of university athletics, or boosters, are of critical importance. Not surprisingly, many NCAA recruitment violations incurred by colleges are directly related to the activities of boosters, because in many instances, they are virtually uncontrolled, often doing whatever may be necessary to acquire the best athletic talent.

Boosters are mobilized interest groups that operate in the sports infrastructure. They are the prime carriers of the corporate ideology that underscores the importance of winning at any cost. Believers in the ideology of commercialization, they identify strongly with winning and exhibit that competitive aggressiveness familiar to Americans in the marketplace as well as in athletics.

Some recent cases in which boosters were implicated in the violation of NCAA recruiting regulations include: giving money to players according to their performance on the field, paying the college costs of the sisters of a potential recruit; use of an apartment for a recruit at a reduced rent, providing free room and board for recruits, providing transportation for recruits, and offering money in exchange for a letter of intent to attend a university.[26]

The influence of boosters is difficult to control. Few university or college presidents have demonstrated the courage of Father Lo Schiavo, president of the University of San Francisco, who in 1982 removed the University's basketball program from Division I ranks. He declared publicly that the university could no longer control its powerful booster organization, and that "there was no way to measure the damage done to the university's most priceless assets, its integrity and reputation."[25] Yet money talks, and booster money talks loudly, even at the University of San Francisco, and recent events at the University of San Francisco should dispel any doubts. The Don Century Club, numbering among its members people of wealth and influence in San Francisco, has apparently forced the reinstatement of basketball at the university.

Perhaps the real issue was not whether basketball would reemerge, but when it did, under what conditions and with what controls. Father Lo Schiavo has announced that the program will be reinstated, though under stronger university control. But reacting to the imperatives of the marketplace, the university's powerful booster club apparently is unwilling to stand for athletic mediocrity under any guise. The battle seems joined, and as one leading member of the Don Century Club recently put it, "Lo Schiavo aspires to mediocrity and would never form a selection committee that would bring us the type of coach we need. I hope for the good of the university, Father Lo Schiavo goes."[26] This last statement captures the essence of the situation. Booster organizations build the links between university athletic programs and the business system with its values. The idea of reestablishing the pursuit of, in this case, basketball supremacy, regardless of university restrictions or controls, has little to do with athletic supremacy or academic excellence; rather it is simply a rational response to the norms of the marketplace.

The situation at the University of San Francisco merits close scrutiny. The notion that basketball programs, at least compared to football, are money-makers has become common in the last few years. Television proceeds, in addition to enormously successful national bowl tournaments and NCAA basketball championships, provide the necessary incentives for the University of San Francisco to commit itself to the idea of athletic success.

Lest anyone doubt the growing magnitude of the role of boosters as

sources of additional financial support, recent information concerning donations to member schools in the Atlantic Coast Conference should arrest that
doubt. As a case in point, North Carolina was able to raise $22 million for a
new basketball arena; $1 million of that was provided by donations from
outside sources. Clemson University has raised $4 million during the last two
years and found itself at odds with the NCAA; as a result, the university
could lose up to $2.5 million in television and postseason revenues. The two
elements (boosters and financial support for sports) cannot be separated. For
example, Clemson University has the largest private fund-raising club in the
country, called IPTAY (the I-Pay-Thirty-A-Year-Club), with fifteen thousand
dues-paying members, and the club lists among its contributions to the
university a $250,000 weight room equipped with twenty-six Nautilus
machines.[27]

Similarly, the University of Maryland, eager to become competitive with
its ambitious conference rivals, launched a campaign to fill the seats of its
football stadium. The campaign was supported by a hefty ninety-thousand-
dollar budget, of which forty thousand dollars was paid to Rodney Danger-
field, "the chronically put-upon . . . tie-hugging, brow-mopping, eye-bulging,
neck-squirming" comedian who laments that while "I don't get no respect,
[but] Maryland does."[28] Undoubtedly, the costs incurred today will be made
up in the years ahead.

The fine line between giving money and expecting to influence policy has
been crossed many times, and the proverbial tail easily wags the dog. Table
5–4 presents the total cash revenue reportedly raised by a number of schools
during the 1981–82 school year. From the data listed it would appear that
the successful competition for donations in the Atlantic Coast Conference
appears to outstrip that in other conferences, and one cannot but speculate
that the recent success of Atlantic Coast Conference athletic programs, espe-

## Table 5–4
## The Collegiate Coffers

The following figures came from school officials and represent the amount of cash revenue raised
during the 1981–82 school year. Special fundraisers for athletic facilities, new football fields,
etc., were not included, nor were noncash contributions such as cattle, oil, or land. In some
instances, the colleges kept records according to the calendar year; in those cases, the 1982
figures were used.

| ACC | | Big East Conference | |
|---|---|---|---|
| North Carolina | $5,000,000 | Pittsburgh | $857,000 |
| Clemson | 4,102,069 | Connecticut | 667,269 |
| North Carolina State | 2,200,000 | Syracuse | 259,000 |
| Virginia | 2,200,000 | Boston College | 225,000 |
| Wake Forest | 1,500,000 | Georgetown | 135,000 |
| Maryland | 1,300,000 | St. John's | 65,000 |
| Georgia Tech | 1,250,000 | Seton Hall | 6,000 |
| Duke | 1,000,000 | Providence | NA |
| | | Villanova | NA |

## Table 5-4 (Continued)

| Big Eight Conference | | SWC | |
|---|---|---|---|
| Missouri | $4,887,168[a] | Arkansas | $2,750,000 |
| Oklahoma State | 1,900,000 | Texas A&M | 1,500,000 |
| Kansas State | 1,500,000 | Texas Tech | 1,500,000 |
| Kansas | 1,323,342 | SMU | 1,200,000 |
| Iowa State | 1,100,000 | Houston | 750,000 |
| Oklahoma | 1,024,000[b] | Texas | 600,000 |
| Colorado | 900,000 | Rice | 522,419 |
| Nebraska | 700,000 | TCU | 403,092 |
| Big Ten Conference | | Baylor | 200,000 |
| Iowa | $2,650,000 | WAC | |
| Illinois | 1,800,000 | Texas-El Paso | $530,000 |
| Wisconsin | 1,445,000 | New Mexico | 492,274 |
| Indiana | 1,414,273 | Wyoming | 405,000 |
| Ohio State | 1,400,000 | San Diego State | 340,257 |
| Michigan State | 1,129,719 | Colorado State | 250,000 |
| Purdue | 800,000 | Air Force | 135,000 |
| Michigan | 650,000 | Brigham Young | NA |
| Minnesota | 500,000[c] | Hawaii | NA |
| Northwestern | 300,000 | Utah | NA |
| PAC-10 Conference | | Others | |
| Stanford | $3,489,000 | Notre Dame | $8,900,000[d] |
| California | 2,156,897 | South Carolina | 2,800,000 |
| Washington | 2,000,000 | Florida State | 2,000,000 |
| USC | 2,000,000 | Penn State | 1,509,552 |
| Arizona State | 1,500,000 | West Virginia | 1,400,000 |
| Oregon State | 1,060,000 | Richmond | 923,000 |
| Arizona | 700,000 | Virginia Tech | 735,000 |
| Washington State | 700,000 | Tulane | 700,000 |
| UCLA | 600,000 | William and Mary | 622,000 |
| Oregon | 440,000 | Cincinnati | 600,000 |
| SEC | | Louisville | 551,000 |
| | | East Carolina | 550,000 |
| Auburn | $1,800,000 | Rutgers | 485,000 |
| Mississippi State | 1,003,000 | Southern Mississippi | 284,000 |
| Tennessee | 900,000 | Army | 257,000 |
| Kentucky | 874,000 | Memphis State | 255,000 |
| LSU | 781,358 | Bradley | 213,000 |
| Mississippi | 775,000 | Boston University | 115,000 |
| Alabama | NA | Navy | 111,000[e] |
| | | Colgate | 71,000 |
| | | Holy Cross | No booster |
| | | Miami (Fla.) | NA |

Source: *Boston Globe,* July 5, 1983. Compiled by Jeff Pike, Jeff Horrigan, Jocelyn Taub, Dan Novak, Jim Trager, Cathy Cusmano, and Scott Newman.

[a]Includes $3.4 million endowment from deceased alumnus, which became active 1981–82.

[b]Oklahoma boosters also donate cattle, which is not included in the figure.

[c]In addition to its overall booster money, Minnesota basketball and football have separate fundraisers. The figure listed represents just the overall booster contributions.

[d]Notre Dame does not have a booster organization but conducted a one-time endowment fundraiser for nonrevenue-producing sports from September 1981 to December 1982. From its conception until the end of the school year in June 1982, the figure was $8.9 million. Through November, the school raised $10.9 million.

[e]Navy relies on regular dues-paying contributors rather than a booster club.

cially two successive years with ACC teams winning the NCAA basketball championship, may somehow be connected with booster support for their athletic programs. The process is a circular one: Generating funds to build athletic facilities and to recruit athletes increases the chances of developing a winning program, which in turn generates the enthusiasm that increases donations.

## Television as a Source of Revenue

Of all of the revenue-generating sources for college athletics none has had the dramatic impact of television. The general social impact of television has been discussed in the preceding chapter, so this chapter will focus on the competition for positional goods and on the financial rewards gained by the universities and colleges that acquire elite status in the production of football and basketball as mass entertainment.

The NCAA limits a university's regular season football appearances over a two-year period to five games. Bowl games do not count. Besides permitting relatively few universities and colleges an opportunity to earn television revenue, NCAA rules also give television producers leeway in the casting of their sports spectaculars. In other words, the networks are able to choose those matchups that will attract the largest television audiences. Within this context, then, it comes as no surprise that teams like those representing Notre Dame, Oklahoma, Penn State, and the University of Alabama appear on television more often than the teams of schools like Kansas or Vanderbilt.

Basketball is not bound by the same NCAA restrictions concerning television appearances as football. Individual universities and colleges, as well as their conferences, retain the right to organize their own regular season television packages. This practice helps to avoid the kind of disputes common in football between the rich, powerful programs and the smaller, less well-known athletic programs that now plague the NCAA.

Basketball attendance has grown as the quality of competition between schools has improved markedly. The long-time "have nots" can attract high quality athletes at a relatively low cost, at least compared to football. This improvement has occurred because basketball, since the televising in 1968 of the first matchup between top-rated UCLA and third-rated University of Houston, has become more visible to a national audience.

To put the symbiotic relationship between national television networks and college sports into perspective, consider that the American Broadcasting System, ABC, paid $225 million for the telecasting rights to the 1984 Olympics. As early as a full year before the actual televising of the Olympics, approximately 90 percent of the advertising, equalling $650 million, at prices of up to $250,000 for a thirty-second prime time advertising spot, had been sold.[29] These figures represent a part of the same corporate-media-sports system that allows the University of Michigan to spend $1 million on its football programs, anticipating that from football alone gate receipts and television income will total approximately $9 million. This same system will enable the Atlantic Coast Conference to increase its television revenues from basketball from $600,000 to $6 million in four seasons.[30]

From this evidence, there seems little doubt that professional football has become the cornerstone of network sports, or that television is socializing the largest audiences. For example, the 1974 radio and television rights for major league basketball amounted to $43.2 million. By contrast, in 1983, largely because of regional and pay TV networks, the amounts rose to an astronomical $153.6 million.[31]

The expansion of professional sports markets has had dramatic effects on the finances of individual universities. The University of North Carolina's fortunes rose dramatically when its team won the 1980–81 NCAA basketball crown, with its total income from commercial television in that year equalling $393,000. During the year 1983–84, the Tarheels are expected to realize $1.5 million from that source.

Some fear that commercial television may be unable to maintain its production schedule in the future. While no one knows where the saturation point exists in the televising of sports, the potential of new pay TV channels may bring about that saturation. According to current estimates, as much as 90 percent of future intercollegiate sports revenue may be derived from television.[32]

These predictions of rising television revenues have caused a squabble between the NCAA and the association of the largest sports powers, the College Football Association (CFA). This challenge could undo the NCAA in its present form, for literally millions of dollars are at stake as the CFA tries to negotiate separate deals with television networks. Besides negotiating its own television contracts, the CFA appears set to push for more televising of its members' games during early afternoon, late afternoon, and evening, its basic justification being that the NCAA allocates too much money to smaller schools. Dan Canham, athletic director at the University of Michigan, a member of the CFA, asserts that the NCAA will be put out of business, with the small schools being hurt the most, if funds continue to be distributed in the present manner. For the record, the University of Michigan athletic program supports five hundred athletes in twenty-one varsity sports, eleven for men and ten for women. Football, as stated earlier, generates $9 million for the University of Michigan; basketball, $1.5 million; other revenue comes from fund raising and hockey.[33]

In many ways the marriage between college basketball and television is even more dramatic than that between television and football. Basketball had been considered "nowhereville" among television sports producers until in 1968 Eddie Einhorn introduced a new epoch with the matchup between UCLA and the University of Houston in the Astrodome before a sellout crowd. High ratings for the event indicated that spectator interest was intense. In the next season, the National Broadcasting Corporation first televised the NCAA championship, and by 1973, the NCAA finals had been moved to prime time Monday night. Within two years, regular season games were shown on Saturday and Sunday. As television coverage increased, the NCAA expanded the tournament field from thirty-two to forty-eight teams and then to sixty-four.

Other television stations, CBS, ESPN, USAM, Metro Sports, and outlets joined NBC and now televise college basketball. As a result, Dean Smith, head basketball coach at North Carolina, noted that his father "in Kansas will be able to see all but four of the Tarheels' twenty-six games."[34] Television dollars induced good basketball teams to seek out the best possible competition in order to enhance their spectator appeal. In general, good teams are searching out other highly rated teams. Since the NCAA playoff field has expanded, teams no longer have to win twenty or more games to qualify for regional or national tournaments, and by the same token, coaches are not afraid to play tough opponents. According to Digger Phelps, head basketball coach at Notre Dame, "I want fourteen power games, eleven got-to-win games, and two others that can go either way but aren't considered power games. If you can win 50 percent of your power games and all the rest, you have a twenty-victory season. It's called marketing."[35]

Estimated television revenues for Division I basketball games in 1984 totaled around $35 million. A few college programs expect to generate more television income than any professional franchise. Programs like those at Kentucky, Georgetown, Houston, North Carolina, and UCLA, for example, all generate more television income than any NBA franchise. The Southeast Conference has received a great boost with television contracts totaling $20 to $21 million during the next three years. Furthermore, Anheuser-Busch, a heavy investor, is committed to joint ventures to carry Southwest Conference basketball games and in a few years will start its own regional pay television network.[36] Such regional networks may be the forerunners of a national pay-view service encompassing all major sports.

The amount of money involved is enormous. With high network ratings in 1981, executives projected that 631 million people would watch college football on ABC and CBS in 1982, up 12.2 percent from 1981. Additionally, the networks were to pay an extra $5 million in rights fees in 1983 to the Turner Broadcasting Service, an increase of nearly $3 million. From a purely financial point of view, much was at stake.[37]

The challenges to network power over college sports increased as did the money. Many believed that if the suit by the Universities of Georgia and Oklahoma were successful, universities could become independent entrepreneurs and an immediate glut on the sports production market would take place.[38] A scramble to present live coverage on national, regional, and cable television would take place. One view projected the unraveling of national network coverage, that is, fewer national telecasts, which would involve the risk of losing contact with the New York advertising community, "where networks' sales forces sell national programs to national advertisers for large sums."[39]

According to its football television committee, the NCAA has a good record in developing a sport whose attendance rose from 17 million in 1952, the first year of full television coverage, to approximately 36.5 million in 1982 for all levels of intercollegiate football. The regulated telecasting of intercollegiate football was largely responsible for this growth. From the three successful series of college football telecasts aired in 1982, NCAA members received $66.4 million. Local telecasts generated additional revenue, extending the number of colleges and universities appearing on television to 165. Of this total, seventy-six were on either the ABC or CBS football series, and add to this number the fourteen colleges that participated in a prime-time supplementary series for the Turner Broadcasting System.[40]

The NCAA has not ignored the role of television in college sports. One of the most important matters taken up at its 1983 annual meeting was the future role of NCAA in the telecasting of intercollegiate football. The Burciaga decision in September of 1982 determined that the existing NCAA television plan, and the network contracts entered into pursuant to that plan, constituted an unlawful restraint of trade in violation of Section 1 of the Sherman Antitrust Act and an unlawful monopolization of the pertinent market, violating Section 2. To many of the delegates at the convention, this ruling imperiled the association's television program.[41] At stake were television contracts projected for 1985 totaling $234 million and the structure of the organization itself.

The economics of television dictates that advertisers want national coverage with predictable outcomes. Anything that involves uncertainty and risk in recouping investment or that threatens profits is avoided. Intercollegiate football as it is presently organized has a ratings history that promises a profitable venture for everyone, but some advertisers worry that college football may cease to be a "prime time television affair."[42]

Another fear is that the effects of falling television ratings will cause a ripple effect on live spectator attendances. If television ratings were to decline to the point where large numbers of fans ceased to attend games, more than a few universities and colleges might decide to cut or reduce the level of intercollegiate sports competition. The NCAA believes that a positive relationship exists between the growth in the televising of football games and the increase in attendance. While television revenues have grown in importance, they are still dwarfed by gate revenues. If one assumes an average ticket price of eight dollars for Division I and II games in 1982, then gate receipts would exceed $243 million, while only $66.4 million would come from television.[43] It is difficult to predict at this point the various fronts on which the NCAA will fight to preserve its regulatory prerogatives to control the televising of intercollegiate football. Undoubtedly, the matter will proceed through the judicial system culminating, perhaps, in a Supreme Court decision. Some believe that the NCAA through its membership and council might seek legislative support for exemption from the Sherman Act,[44] and although such a course would be difficult, it could succeed.

Professional sports leagues have over the years obtained basic legislative exemptions for many of their activities. In fact, in 1982 the National Football League used legislative support in Congress to overturn a federal court decision, based on Sherman Act principles, voiding the NFL's contractual restraints on franchise shifts. There was considerable support in Congress for the measure, suggesting the possibility of some cooperation between the professional franchises and the NCAA, particularly if the exemptions were to cover the NCAA's football television plan or other NCAA-sanctioned arrangements. Much of this is speculation, but there is every reason to believe that the matter is far from closed and that political options will be pursued.

### Television Revenues and Post-season Football Games

Television's impact on college sports, especially on college football, has profoundly affected the financial structure of those sports, a fact dramatically illustrated by the annual matchups for postseason bowl games. Table 5–5 shows the outline of 1983 bowl games.

No decline in football revenues seems to have occurred according to a survey of television revenues by schools participating in NCAA-sanctioned postseason bowl games. Gross receipts for the thirty-two competing schools in 1982 reached approximately $35 million; of this amount $27 million was distributed to the participating schools, a sharp increase from the $4 million of the previous year.[45] The Southeast Conference was most frequently represented in bowl games, garnering $5.5 million in revenues. Furthermore, each of the seven SEC schools that did not go to bowls (Mississippi, Mississippi State, and Kentucky) collected $250,000 under the conference's revenue-sharing agreement.[46]

The only bowl failing to increase its total revenues was the Blue Bonnet Bowl. In 1982, it paid $300,000 to each participating school. In the previous year, revenues were $902,000. The NCAA was projecting a minimum of $400,000 in earnings for each school in the 1983 postseason bowl games.[47] Teams selected to participate in so-called major bowls anticipate earnings of $1 million each.[48]

**Table 5–5**
**1983 Bowl Game Matchups**

| Bowl | Date | Time (EST) | Location | TV | Teams | 1981 Funds |
|---|---|---|---|---|---|---|
| Aloha | Dec. 25 | 7 P.M. | Honolulu, HI | ESPN | Maryland *vs.* UCLA or Washington | NA |
| Bluebonnet | Dec. 31 | 8 P.M. | Houston, TX | ESPN | Arkansas *vs.* Florida | $902,000 |
| California | Dec. 18 | 4 P.M. | Fresno, CA | ESPN | Bowling Green *vs.* Fresno State | NA |
| Cotton | Jan. 1 | 2 P.M. | Dallas, TX | CBS | Pittsburgh *vs.* Southern Methodist | $3,260,082 |
| Fiesta | Jan. 1 | 1:30 P.M. | Tempe, AZ | NBC | Arizona State or Washington *vs.* Nebraska or Oklahoma | $1,750,000 |
| Gator | Dec. 30 | 9 P.M. | Jacksonville, FL | ABC | Florida State *vs.* West Virginia | $1,022,498 |
| Hall of Fame | Dec. 31 | 2 P.M. | Birmingham, AL | ESPN | Air Force *vs.* Vanderbilt | $800,000 |
| Holiday | Dec. 17 | 9 P.M. | San Diego, CA | ESPN | Brigham Young *vs.* Ohio State | $572,358 |
| Independence | Dec. 11 | 8 P.M. | Shreveport, LA | ESPN | Kansas States *vs.* Wisconsin | $436,266 |
| Liberty | Dec. 29 | 8 P.M. | Memphis, TN | ESPN | Alabama *vs.* Illinois | $819,734 |
| Orange | Jan. 1 | 8 P.M. | Miami, FL | NBC | Luisiana State *vs.* Nebraska or Oklahoma | $3,076,848 |
| Peach | Dec. 31 | 3 P.M. | Atlanta, GA | CBS | Iowa *vs.* Tennessee | $753,239 |
| Rose | Jan. 1 | 5 P.M. | Pasadena, CA | NBC | Michigan *vs.* Arizona State or UCLA | $5,733,126 |
| Sugar | Jan. 1 | 8 P.M. | New Orleans, LA | ABC | Georgia *vs.* Penn State | $2,642,000 |
| Sun | Dec. 25 | 3 P.M. | El Paso, TX | CBS | North Carolina *vs.* Texas | $650,000 |
| Tangerine | Dec. 18 | 8 P.M. | Orlando, FL | ESPN | Auburn *vs.* Boston College | $610,000 |

Source: *Chronicle of Higher Education*—Athletics.
Note: ESPN—Entertainment Sports Programming Network; 1981 funds–amounts divided between teams.

Appearances in bowl games in addition to being financially profitable also provide universities with free advertisements in the form of extensive media exposure. Bowl games also enhance the image of a university: the NCAA offers special profiles during such events of the academic programs and achievements of participating universities. These appearances also have a salutory effect on the university's athletic programs' recruitment efforts.

The selection process for these money-makers reveals how influential television producers have become in college sports. With the exception of the Rose Bowl, which matches the Pacific Ten Conference champions with the Big Ten Conference champions, and the California Bowl, which matches the Pacific Coast Athletic Association champions with the Mid-American Athletic Conference champions, officers of major bowls are relatively free to select team participants. For example, the Orange, Cotton, and Sugar Bowls use a reserve selection system. At least one participant in those bowls includes the conference winner of the Big Eight, the Southwestern, and the Southeastern Conferences, respectively. Other bowls have *carte blanche* in selecting their participants. Most bowls are owned and operated by nonprofit corporations.[49]

A team's "attractiveness" to a national television audience is among the most important criteria used to select participants. Merely having a winning record for the season does not necessarily assure a bowl berth for a team. The team must also attract either a large stadium crowd or a sizable television audience. Strong sports traditions, an outstanding athlete with media appeal, a winning record, and a television following all contribute to the attractiveness of a team before a national television audience. Vince Lombardi was wrong: winning is not the only thing; rather, winning and attracting a large television audience are the only things!

Bowl officials invite intense political lobbying for the lucrative bowl bids from postseason hopefuls, in effect "politicizing" the selection process. Much of this pressure for a bowl bid would disappear if a systematic way of selecting a national collegiate football champion actually existed. As the situation now stands, an "official" champion is selected at the end of the season after all bowl games have been played, and this system allows for wide discretion in the definition of attractive bowl participants.

A former commissioner of the Missouri Valley Conference articulated a sense of the "agony of defeat" in the matter of selection for bowl games when he stated: "You think you've got a very qualified team but nobody seems interested. So you just keep trying to get the bowl committees to watch them, and keep trying to get them interested."[50] Getting to one of the prestigious bowl games earns the participants a considerable windfall of television revenues and also creates a favorable image of the teams playing as well as of the conferences they represent. Additionally, money and success tend to beget more money and success. To put the matter bluntly, a successful bowl appearance goes a long way in prying open the pocketbooks of alumni and booster groups, even evidently when it comes to supporting nonathletic activities.

A bowl appearance also gains for the university the benefits of free publicity generated by media exposure. The specific events also influence the media outcomes. Peak events, such as regional rivalries, conference championships, or bowl appearances virtually guarantee an intensely committed viewing audience. In these situations, television functions as a catalytic agent, activating symbols that heighten and intensify spectator identification with the university, and not surprisingly, these processes help attract prime athletic talent to athletic programs.

Key sports events give a university opportunities to gain political resources. In connection with such events a university president may establish or strengthen ties to local politicians, businessmen, alumni, and other contacts in the community. Such political contacts do not necessarily bring immediate increases in the university's budget, but the influence of such contacts constitutes an aspect of systemic power. These contacts enable the university over the long run to merge discrete interests into a coherent set of unified interests politically available to support special, large-scale university projects. As the university nurtures these contacts via sports events, the distinction between the university's values and corporate values diminishes, with the result that universities and the business world become more interdependent. In short, systemic power reinforced through television helps universities to elicit the political support of key clientele.

## Conclusion

Assessing the financial and economic aspects of intercollegiate sports is at best difficult and subject to considerable confusion. We have tried to determine from the mass of information what appear to us to be the most important economic indicators of corporate athleticism, and we will sum them up here.

Relatively few universities have financially self-supporting sports programs. The real costs of sports programs are probably inflated, and many presidents lack the time to develop cost-effective controls over sports expenditures. Expenditures for the sports program are frequently settled upon through informal bargaining, outside the normal budgetary processes of the university.

Rich universities are getting richer in big-time sports. Public universities are likely to compound their advantages in recruitment with state financial support, and with the size of their student bodies, they will consequently assume most of the production of sports events. If economies of scale exist in college sports, the large public universities are well positioned economically to take advantage of them.

Traditional sources of revenue for sports programs have remained stable, but receipts from television sources are increasing substantially. Unearned income from state assistance and from booster contributions provides an increasingly large share of income to athletic departments. This trend will probably continue and should grow in importance in coming years.

In view of current national economic trends, the ability of the university to finance sports programs will probably remain uncertain. Television revenues may become somewhat uncertain because of the crowding of sports events on television, and this trend may alter the benefits calculations of prime advertisers regarding the value of their sponsorship. Political limits on athletic departments are being established through efforts to increase presidential control over the NCAA, and economic limits are appearing as the number of sports events presented on television grows. Media saturation fragments markets and heightens spectator reaction to the explicitly commercial aspects of sports.

The economic incentive associated with corporate athleticism has its own dynamic, in that market forces define a structure of incentives that universities find difficult to ignore. Regardless of their educational missions, universities experience financial constraints that induce them to respond positively to market forces and as a result their relationship to the economic system is fundamentally changed.

How does this causation at the university level create economic dependence on sports? Changing economic environments compel universities to make careful choices in matters of student access, faculty tenure, and all resource allocation issues. The general decline in the external economic environment quickens the pace at which market forces are integrated into the university. Consequently, universities are more inclined to make allocation choices on the basis of economic rationality or demand criteria. Accordingly, those sports that are not money-making ventures are more likely to be eliminated as educators shift more resources into the money-making sports, thus reinforcing the strength of economic forces in the educational management of sports programs.

We think that political limits have affected the way corporate athleticism has grown. The universities and the NCAA did not clearly define political limits on the penetration of market phenomena into the university. Both were enticed by the economic resources to be gained from corporate athleticism. But more recently, political pressures to control economic forces in the athletic department have grown because of the explicit threat to presidential authority now posed by the corporate athletic complex.

Commodity development as a critical input in economic production is unequally distributed geographically. The cost of competition for scarce athletic talent, especially in football, will enhance the relatively strong market position of certain universities. Despite efforts at regulatory control, universities have become more mobilized in their efforts to compete for athletic talent, and as we have seen, these competitive economic pressures to some extent affect the geographic distribution of NCAA violations. Universities with a less favorably endowed market position are more likely to engage in special efforts, that is, to use illegal means, to compete for athletic talent.

We see presidential authority working on an integrated constituency model. As university presidents lose the ability to control the institution internally, they will have relatively fewer options. This internal political constraint prompts presidents to try to extend their power beyond the university to integrate it through an external constituency, by building countervailing constituencies outside the university itself. In this way, the president gains contextual power, as can be seen in the presidential efforts to control the NCAA through the forty-four-member presidential council. Considering the dense interest-group infrastructure around the athletic department and the high political costs of establishing presidential authority over athletic decision making, presidents have lost internal control over that decision-making arena. Under these conditions, as Schattschneider notes, university presidents now endeavor to socialize the environment and thus enhance their system in power. [51]

All sports do not exist under the same market conditions. Basketball, for example, has a more open market system. The teams have contracts with conferences, more teams are playing at the same time, and more universities of varying size can invest the resources needed to compete in the talent market.

Television is structuring the sports market. Some are concerned about the saturation of the sports television market, the argument being that with crowding of television saturation, product deterioration occurs. The indicator here of product deterioration is the exit of spectators from television viewing. The NCAA television committee fears that college football, for example, will cease to be a prime television affair, and that a decline in demand for television will produce in turn a decline in public spectator attendance. With a decline in the gate audience, the costs of producing live television games would increase. On the face of it, however, these fears do not seem justified by the evidence. Marginal changes in television appearance may occur; some sports will decline, others will become more popular, but the long-term trend is for more segments of the American population to become aware of the advantages of participating in some physical activity. This trend seems likely to produce greater general interest in some form of television sports presentation. Indeed, the fears that television markets will decline are not supported by the evidence. The demand for sports, as we see it, is contingent on alternative time allocations of similar or greater mass appeal, and at present, such alternative time allocations have been invented.

In the Georgia-Oklahoma case, the NCAA may try to mobilize the broader sports lobbies, including the professional sports political lobby, in order to have the NCAA exempted from monopoly rulings. According to this scenario, the NCAA would try to induce Congress to pass legislation making possible for the NCAA an exemption from the Sherman antitrust provisions. It is clear that the issue is far from being resolved, and each side will pull out all the stops to win.

According to our analysis, boosters' involvement in college athletics is going to increase. In time the boosters' involvement will become an accepted feature of athletic organization as other units of the university, like libraries, academic departments, and other university programs, have developed their own support groups; in short, the role of booster groups will come to be perceived as more legitimate. The important question then is how the strengthening of booster clubs will affect the governance structure of the university. These more powerful booster groups will, at first glance, make it more difficult for presidents to control athletic programs on individual campuses, for they will strengthen the political linkages between the athletic departments and local business and alumni interests. Boosters are active, emotional, and financial supporters of sports activity. Their groups are more encompassing than alumni groups, since the boosters also include local business interests. Involvement in booster activity also mobilizes the affective identification of alumni with the university.

Finally, athletic directors will continue to experience conflicting pressures. They have to get the support, at least tacitly, of university administrators, faculty, and students. Gaining this support requires balancing the interests of these elements of the university community, but we believe that the boosters, already a part of the athletic directors' power base, will play an ever more active role. These conditions are exacerbated by changes in the economic situations of universities and colleges.

## Notes

1. John L. Rooney, Jr., *The Recruiting Game* (Lincoln, Neb.: University of Nebraska Press, 1980). See also John L. Rooney, Jr., "Intercollegiate Athletic Recruiting: A Geographical Analysis of Its Origin, Diffusion and Potential Demise," *Phi Kappa Phi Journal* (Winter 1982):32–36.

2. Robert H. Atwell, Bruce Grimes, and Donna A. Lopiano, *The Money Game: Financing Collegiate Athletics* (Washington, D.C.: American Council on Education, 1980), 8.

3. Ibid., 7–8.

4. Ibid., 9; *Wall Street Journal,* 29 Oct. 1982, p. 1.

5. *Sports Illustrated,* 31 August 1981, 13.

6. Mitchell Raiborn, *Revenues and Expenses of Intercollegiate Athletic Pro-*

*grams* (Shawnee Mission, Kans.: National Collegiate Athletic Association, 1978–1982).

7. Atwell et al., *The Money Game,* 10.

8. Ibid., 11; Raiborn, *Revenues and Expenses,* 1982, 15.

9. Class A institutions in 1981 included 187 institutions classified in Division I in football in accordance with the provisions of NCAA bylaws 9 and 10 (1982–83 NCAA Manual).

10. Raiborn, *Revenues and Expenses,* 1982, 15.

11. Atwell et al., *The Money Game,* 12.

12. Raiborn, *Revenues and Expenses,* 16.

13. Raiborn, quoted in the *Wall Street Journal,* 29 Oct. 1982, p. 1.

14. Atwell et al., *The Money Game,* 13.

15. Ibid.

16. Ibid.

17. Rooney, *The Recruiting Game,* 144.

18. Rooney, "Intercollegiate Athletic Recruiting," 33.

19. Ibid.

20. Rooney, *The Recruiting Game,* 75.

21. Ibid.

22. *Sporting News,* 23 May 1983, 33.

23. Ibid.

24. *Wall Street Journal,* 16 Oct. 1980, p. 16.

25. "Boosters as Carriers of Corporate Ideology." *Chronicle of Higher Education,* 26 Oct. 1983, p. 26.

26. *Boston Globe,* 4 July 1983, p. 29.

27. *Sports Illustrated,* 16 Nov. 1981.

28. *Sports Illustrated,* 28 Sept. 1982, 13; Lesley Visser, "Atlantic Coast or Gold Coast?" *Boston Globe,* p. 36.

29. *Washington Post,* 11 July 1983, sec. D, p. 1.

30. Ibid., sec. D, p. 3.

31. Ibid.

32. Ibid.

33. Ibid.

34. *Sports Illustrated,* 30 Nov. 1981, 38.

35. Ibid., 43.

36. *Sporting News,* 4 July 1983, 49.

37. National Collegiate Athletic Association, *1983 Convention Proceedings* (San Diego, Calif.: 1983), 72.

38. Ibid., 73.

39. Ibid., 73–74.

40. Ibid., 71.

41. Ibid., 70.

42. Ibid., 74.

43. Ibid.

44. Ibid., 77.

45. *Sporting News,* 23 May 1983, 50.

46. Ibid.

47. Ibid.

48. N. Scott Vance, "Making It to a Football Bowl Takes More Than a Good Record," *Chronicle of Higher Education* 25 no. 14, 1.

49. Ibid., 16.

50. Ibid.

51. E.E. Schattschneider, *The Semi-Sovereign People* (New York: Holt, Rinehart & Winston, 1960), 103–5.

# 6
# The Politics of Sports Administration

Perhaps because sports is so deeply rooted in American popular culture, it has rarely been the subject of systematic analysis by social science. Serious academic interest in the subject developed in the 1960s, however, when considerable attention was focused on the black athlete as an exploited victim of the sports system. Few academics have devoted specific attention to examining sports administration as it intersects with politics, culture, business, and higher education in ways destined to yield substantial, ideological consequences for American society.

In spite of the widely lamented demise of amateurism in college sports, the NCAA has yet to find an effective way to resolve core regulatory issues pertaining to the organization of college sports. In this chapter, we discuss first the shift in actual control of college sports away from the general university administration as it has taken place since the founding of the NCAA. Although university presidents periodically emphasize—as they have in recent years—the need for regulatory reforms in college sports, they possess few viable political instruments for effecting such reforms. The NCAA has not been effective either in controlling college sports. Since the 1984 Supreme Court decision concerning the NCAA monopoly role in college sports, a second shift in the control of college sports has occurred, heralding the full commercialization of college sports and the final overthrow of the idea of amateurism as an organizing concept for college sports. In light of the de facto delegation of authority for sports administration within the university to highly autonomous athletic directors and coaches, college sports is now under the control of the very people whose commercially-oriented behavior university presidents and the NCAA have unsuccessfully sought to regulate.

Over the years, studies of college sports have warned against the drift toward commercialism—a situation in which business interests, external to the university, rather than educational values constitute the driving force behind college sports. As David Nelson, the University of Delaware's athletic director, paradoxically noted, "The institutions of higher education of the country have been responsible for major discoveries in every discipline but have yet to solve satisfactorily governance problems of intercollegiate athletics. The concerns of administrators, faculty, students, friends, alumni and the public are not much different in 1983 than they were in 1883, 1893, 1903, or 1923."[1] Since those comments were made, corporate athleticism has gained new strength from the Supreme Court ruling. Whereas commercialism was a significant concern in previous academic reports, it has in recent decades become a central element of college sports, thanks to a unique configuration of political forces within both the American university and the NCAA. Nelson's statement also highlights the inherently contradictory nature of political control in college sports. On one level, college sports are widely perceived as an educational endeavor, mainly because of its structural location in American universities and colleges, while simultaneously on another, it is in fact politically controlled through the NCAA, whose regulatory processes are directly and indirectly influenced by specialized economic and political interests.

## The NCAA As Regulator

By and large, the NCAA operates for the regulatees. In most instances, the most powerful of these quasi-institutional interests—such as alumni-organized booster clubs—operate outside the core educational values of higher education and it is these booster groups that are mainly responsible for shaping certain central features of intercollegiate athletics. In contrast, the NCAA's formal role is to monitor intercollegiate athletics within the context of an educational system, clearly differentiating it from professional sports.

The effectiveness of the NCAA in sustaining these standards has been called into question recently by several widely publicized events. For example, intercollegiate athletics has become politicized at two institutions—the University of San Francisco and Villanova University—institutions where strong sports constituencies have effectively applied pressure to reverse presidential decisions to ban football and basketball. In both cases, the presidents were defeated by mobilized alumni sports constituencies. At Villanova, staunch alumni supporters reportedly refused to contribute funds to the university until the Board of Trustees revoked the decision to ban football.[2]

These and other recent issues—namely the proposal to create a forty-four-member presidential board, the Proposition 48 decision, the Georgia–Oklahoma lawsuit against the NCAA—indicate the heightened politicization of college sports. Accordingly, many university presidents who were previously content to leave regulation to the NCAA or to their own athletic directors have decided that they can no longer allow reform to lie solely in the hands of those being regulated.

This increased politicization of college sports may indicate a breakdown of the existing regulatory structure. In several respects, the NCAA faces challenges that, if successful, will restructure its authority. The NCAA currently finds itself involved in issues of race and student recruitment, political autonomy and presidential control, and the right of individual institutions to negotiate contracts with national television producers. Television contracts and the expansion of cable television are drawing the NCAA into the formation of new political-economic relations. College sports is now so deeply involved with the marketplace, and the NCAA seems poorly equipped administratively, politically, and economically to regulate the evolving political economy of intercollegiate sports. As collegiate athletics becomes more closely organized along the lines of professional sports, new actors—national television corporations, individual institutions, individual athletes, player agents, coaches, athletic directors, NCAA staff, cable television networks, and university presidents—all have come to form a modern complex of intercollegiate sports interests that are not yet fully systematized. In the face of changing economic and political conditions, the NCAA's ability to maintain the existing equilibrium without scandal or student athlete rebellion is weak, and as a consequence, the NCAA is enmeshed in political conflicts over the attempt to establish alternative regulatory mechanisms.

Since its inception, the NCAA has confronted issues of the compatibility of intercollegiate sports and the educational objectives of higher education. America has produced a unique set of institutional questions concerning the relationship between sports and higher education. For one thing, the regulation of intercollegiate sports in the United States was complicated at the outset by the commercial context with which intercollegiate sports was associated. Sports was often used to raise public and private funds for the large, land-grant universities. Intercollegiate sports offered legislators a practical benefit for the expenditure of public funds; if pure scientific research could not always generate a large base of legislative support, the existence of a winning tradition in football or basketball could draw favorable attention both to the university and to the legislators. At the same time, intercollegiate sports was a commercial venture, one that helped both public and private universities raise money.

In a real sense, college sports connects the university to mass society and, less visible, to the evolving political culture and values of that mass society; plainly, the political implications of college sports should not be underestimated. The NCAA's persistent governance problems arise to some extent from its having been granted little authority to deal with inherently contradictory goals. Encouraging intercollegiate sports has been perceived as support for academic values, but at the time, such encouragement set the stage for the infusion of commercial value into the formative structures of educational institutions whose primary purpose was and is, like the monestary, to maintain a certain distance from society. It is therefore important to understand how the regulatory structure of the NCAA, contrary to its formal constitutive principles, laid the foundations for the extensive commercialization of intercollegiate sports. At best, the NCAA has maintained a mere semblance of regulatory control, with only meager administrative resources to sanction member institutions' violation of its rules.

One insightful observer offered the following description of the NCAA's institutional malaise:

> The institutional problems existing in intercollegiate ahtletics are well known. The media, educators and the National Collegiate Athletic Association have disclosed numerous abuses: forged transcripts and student athletes' exhausting their years of eligibility without attaining their degrees, for example. Low graduation rates grimly but eloquently attest to the discordant values operating in intercollegiate athletics.[3]

The American Council on Education (ACE) reform perspective also contends that the NCAA has failed to clearly differentiate college athletics from professional sports. Instead, athleticism—or the values associated with commercial athletic interests—now dominates university decision making with respect to college sports. This has occurred because some NCAA policies actually blur the separation between education and athletics, making it more difficult to distinguish between college and professional sports.

One alternative is offered by the ACE, which is critical of the weak regulatory performance by the NCAA. To correct this situation the ACE recently proposed unsuccessfully before the NCAA that a forty-four-man board of university presidents be formed and that this board be given veto power over many NCAA rules. In the proposal, the ACE argues that reform measures would recouple (that is, centralize) the processes of political and administrative control, substantially reducing the amount of political autonomy that educational authorities previously granted to the athletic directors of their intercollegiate sports programs. The ACE proposal assumes that the forty-four-man board of presidents could muster the political resources to stabilize the governance structure of the NCAA through *collective* presidential rule. This mechanism might act as a more potent control than the existing system of presidential leadership on individual college and university campuses. The presidential board "would have the right to suspend any NCAA rule that significantly affects the academic standards, the financial integrity or the reputation of the member institutions."[4]

Historically, the ACE proposal turns the NCAA regulatory issue around. Universities originally granted the NCAA regulatory authority in 1906 so that each campus would not have to regulate intercollegiate sports individually. But faculty and administrators have remained largely indifferent to the intercollegiate sports association for more than half a century. Many university officials seem to recognize that, because of their extremely fragmented internal authority structure, universities are ill-equipped to administer intercollegiate sports. The ACE secondary hypothesis, as formulated by Jack Peltason, a recent past president of the ACE and a former chancellor at the University of Illinois, rightly argues that, "Our problem is not with enforcement of the rules. Our problem is with the rules as they now exist. Athletics get so emphasized that even if teams abide by the rules, it is difficult for a person to get a college education and participate in an intercollegiate athletic program."[5]

## Scandal and Administrative Reform

The number of proposals for administrative reform of intercollegiate sports increased during the 1970s. Two factors shaped the evolving context of the NCAA's reform efforts: first, several nationally commissioned studies on education in the sciences, in mathematics, and in the core curriculum of the public schools; and second, a series of scandals at several Division I football and basketball schools underscored the need to devise new mechanisms of administrative control for NCAA member organizations. Violations of NCAA procedures included special payments or in-kind gifts to induce highly touted high school athletes to attend specific institutions. As of 1983, eighteen colleges and universities were under sanctions by the NCAA.

Table 6–1 documents the violations of the NCAA rules, and the penalties meted out. Of the eighteen universities sanctioned by the NCAA, most were located in the South (seven), the Southwest (five), and the West (five); only one team was located in the Midwest, and no teams in the Northeast were sanctioned. For the most part, sanctions of one or two years' duration were meted out to universities, mostly in Division I or I-A. Of the teams sanctioned, nine were prohibited from participating in postseason bowls for one or two years. Eight universities received no sanctions for violations involving booster payments to athletes, though two universities had their grants for athletic scholarships reduced. In addition, the NCAA denied permission to nine universities to appear on television for at lest one year or more.

In fifteen of the eighteen cases, rule infractions mainly involved direct booster payments to athletes, or indirect, in-kind gifts or booster payments to a member of an athlete's family. To reduce these infractions, the NCAA adopted rules with stricter penalties for coaches or boosters who offered unauthorized material inducements to young athletes. On the face of it, the new rules to control coaches and boosters, as well as the institutional sanctions, seem relatively mild, in view of the substantial bowl receipts and television payments involved. More substantive NCAA rules were devised to tighten academic requirements for student athletes. With the support of the

# Table 6-1
## The NCAA Violaters: How Boosters Played a Part

Dave Berst, director of enforcement for the National Collegiate Athletic Assn., recently said that all the recruiting violations that have been handed down over the years, he can think of none in which booster had either direct or indirect influence. The indirect influences sometimes are hard to prove: For instance, if a school's assistant coach gives a recruit money to attend the school, the money most likely didn't come out of the assistant coach's pocket; instead, it came from a booster or a booster club fund. The school would go on probation if the NCAA could prove that the assistant coach gave the recruit money; the NCAA would get an extra feather in its cap if it could trace that money to its source, but it's not mandatory to do that to get the school on probation. However, direct influences of boosters have been uncovered. Of the 18 programs currently on probation, 16 have been penalized for at least one by-law violation broken specifically by a booster. Of the total 208 by-laws broken by the 18 colleges, 65—or 32 percent—directly involve boosters.

| Institution (Division) | Date Penalty Imposed | Date Penalty to End | Sport | Sanctions in Effect | (Number of direct booster violations); More Flagrant Violations |
|---|---|---|---|---|---|
| University of New Mexico (1) | 11/28/80 | 11/28/84 | bkb | none | (10) Basketball player given money according to number of rebounds he got in two games; Lobo booster club gave athletic director a $10,000 fund. |
| Clemson University (1-A) | 11/21/82 | 11/21/84 | fb | no bowl '82, '83; no TV '83, '84; 10 grants cut '83–84 and '84–85 | (9) Booster offered to pay the costs for two sisters of a recruit to attend the university |
| University of Miami (Fla.) (1-A) | 11/2/81 | 11/2/83 | fb | none | (9) Booster gave player money according to player's performance on the field |
| University of Arizona (1-A) | 5/19/83 | 5/19/85 | fb | no bowl '83, '84; no TV '84, '85 | (7) Executive director of booster club provided cash to administrators and coaches to pay educational, recruiting and supplemental costs as well as extra benefits to athletes |
| University of Southern Miss. (1-A) | 10/25/82 | 10/25/84 | fb | no bowl '82, '83; no TV '83, '84 | (6) Booster offered a recruit a substantial amount of money to sign a letter of commitment to attend Southern Mississippi and an even larger amount if the recruit signed a national letter of intent |
| Arkansas State University (1) | 10/15/81 | 10/15/83 | bkb | none | (6) Booster offered to arrange for a recruit to be provided a car |
| UCLA (1) | 12/4/81 | 12/4/83 | bkb | none | (4) Booster allowed a player to use his apartment at reduced rent |

| | | | | | |
|---|---|---|---|---|---|
| North Carolina St. Univ. (1-A) | 3/3/83 | 3/3/84 | fb | none | (3) A recruit was provided transportation on various occasions, as well as lodging and meals for one night |
| University of Oregon (fb 1-A; bkb 1) | 12/22/81 | 12/22/83 | fb, bkb | no bowl or TV '82 | (3) Boosters provided free room and board for recruits and free meals for Oregon athletes at a Eugene, OR restaurant |
| Wichita State University (1) | 12/18/81 | 12/18/84 | bkb, fb | no postseason, 1 grant cut, '82–83 bkb; no bowl or TV '83, '84 fb | (2) Boosters provided round-trip automobile transportation to a recruit |
| University of Georgia (1-A) | 9/17/82 | 9/17/83 | fb | 3 grant cuts '83–84 | (1) Booster gave a player a check that said 'Christmas gift' on it, although it seemed to represent deferred payment for summer employment at a rate in excess of the job performed |
| University of Southern Calif. (1-A) | 4/22/82 | 4/22/85 | fb | no bowl '82, '83; no TV '83, '84 | (1) Boosters—16 have been identified—bought allotments of players' complimentary football tickets ranging in value from $400 to $2000 |
| University of Texas (1-A) | 9/22/82 | 9/22/83 | fb | none | (1) Booster purchased 14 complimentary football tickets from a player at a price substantially in excess of their face value |
| Oklahoma City University (1) | 12/14/82 | 12/14/84 | bkb | no postseason or TV '82–83 | (1) Booster received a round-trip airline ticket to accompany a recruit on the recruit's paid visit |
| Florida State University (1) | 3/4/83 | 3/4/84 | bkb | none | (1) Two boosters paid for an athlete's suit |
| Virginia Tech (1-A) | 5/16/83 | 5/16/84 | fb | none | (1) Booster gave a recruit and his parents a load of firewood |
| University of San Diego (3) | 12/22/82 | 12/22/83 | fb | no bowl or TV '83–84 | (0) No booster-related violations |
| Western State College (2) | 9/1/82 | 9/1/84 | all sports | no postseason or TV '82–83 all sports; no postseason '83–84 fb | (0) No booster-related violations |

Source: *Boston Globe*, July 3, 1983.

American Council on Education, a panel of twenty college presidents was formed to "insure that student-athletes are bona fide students, receiving the kind of education, the univesities [say] they're giving them."[6] Although previously some educators had expressed concern about the possible adverse effects of sports commercialization on colleges and universities, this theme was noticeably missing from the most recent NCAA debates.[7] Instead, the most prominent theme at the 1983 convention meetings was the recruitment of student-athletes, whose sports service to universities was not accompanied by the education of such students at the college level. Hence, NCAA regulations should be altered so that student-athletes would, like other students, be capable of performing as regular college students.

## The Student-Athlete As Exploited Agent

One consistent theme in the NCAA political discourse involves the assertion that universities have abused the athletic talents of students who are unable to perform as college students. Since many such students fail to make normal progress toward attaining college degrees, student-athletes may have little to show for their many years in college; such students are deemed exploited agents. To improve the terms of trade between universities and athletes, the NCAA, at its January 1983 meeting in San Diego, passed Proposition 48 on freshmen recruitment, calling for more stringent academic standards. Unless such rules are adopted, one university president argued, a permanent subclass of students playing intercollegiate sports may develop.[8] At present, student-athletes increasingly function as public entertainers, whose actions elicit media attention as well as huge financial rewards for many NCAA Division I universities.[9]

The increased participation of low-income black athletes in college sports can enhance the social mobility of such individuals. These students are particularly sensitive to booster payments, given their deprived family status. Like others before them, some low-income young people probably attend college more because of their athletic skills than their academic abilities. In addition, the genuine financial needs of many low-income students make them particularly vulnerable to the pecuniary inducements offered by enthusiastic boosters.[10]

At the same time, such athletes may possess severe educational deficits. Although participation in sports may increase the ambition of lower-income students to attend college, their family structures or peer groups seem generally less supportive of high academic achievement.[11] Many lower-income students proceed through college without gaining basic educational skills.[12] Since only a small number of athletes eventually play in the professional leagues, the many athletes who fail as college students are left unprepared to pursue nonathletic careers. According to one report, 174 of 401 college seniors (43.4 percent) who were regulars on their 1980–81 basketball teams had obtained their diplomas as of the fall 1982. Table 6–2 shows graduation rates of basketball players in some of the major athletic conferences. It seems evident that the strongest basketball conferences—the Atlantic Coast and Big Ten—had the lowest graduation rates.

Despite the statistics, it should be noted that, on balance, the graduation rates of athletes compare favorably with normal student rates, although variations in graduation rates in the different athletic conferences appear to be greater than the variation in the graduation rates among the average students. For example, although only 17 percent of the starting seniors in basketball in the Southwest Conference graduated, Rice University, a small, private, elite school in the Southwest Conference, graduates nearly 75 percent of all its athletes.[13] In short, the acadmic values of particular conferences or of individual schools may vary dramatically and may substantially influence graduation rates of athletes. To the extent that the graduation rate of athletes at a particular school or in a particular conference is high, it seems clear that the values of amateurism are sustained in sports. Conversely, if the graduation rates of athletes in a conference or at a university are low, certain elements of corporate athleticism may well be present, distorting academic standards. In other words, the traditions of Rice and Northwestern Universities suggest that a university's high academic standards may reinforce an athlete's academic productivity and his educational outcomes more generally.

The relatively low (43.4 percent) graduation rate for basketball regulars in select conferences seems only partially related to educational deficiencies; it also seems to be related to the more intense competitive pressures found, for example, in the Atlantic Coast and Big Ten—two athletically-oriented conferences. The lower the graduation rates, other things being equal, the more likely it is that athletes are being treated as market commodities rather than as students. In part, the rate of black participation in intercollegiate sports did and could increase rapidly because academic criteria were not applied: athletes were perceived simply as market agents, not as students. This willingness of some universities to suspend academic criteria for athletes merely underlines how deeply market forces penetrated intercollegiate athletics in many NCAA Division I schools.

Another important economic agent of such market penetration is the booster or alumni clubs. Many of these clubs raise funds for student-athlete scholarships, for the athletic departments' operating costs, or for supplements to a coach's salary. These activities, if successfully organized, may generate considerable financial resources for a sports program. Because of their persistent violation of NCAA athletic recruitment policies, alumni groups are frequently said to be out of control: they repeatedly violate NCAA recruitment policies through cash or in-kind payments, such as summer jobs,

**Table 6–2**
**Graduation Rates of Basketball Players**

Over all, 174 of 401 seniors (43.4 percent) who were regulars on their basketball teams last year had obtained their diplomas by this fall. Here are the graduation rates of some of the major *athletic conferences* according to the survey.

| Conference | Percentage | Number |
|---|---|---|
| Ivy League | 100.0 | (12 of 12) |
| Big East | 77.3 | (17 of 22) |
| Southern | 63.2 | (12 of 19) |
| Big 8 | 50.0 | (12 of 24) |
| Pacific 10 | 40.7 | (11 of 27) |
| Southeastern | 40.0 | (4 of 10) |
| Atlantic Coast | 36.8 | (7 of 19) |
| Big 10 | 30.4 | (7 of 23) |

Source: *The Chronicle of Higher Education,* (November 3, 1982, p. 17).

cars, and use of credit cards, to highly talented athletes. More generally, booster clubs may raise endowment funds, and these funds represent an important component of corporate athleticism in the competitive world of big-time intercollegiate athletics. In functional terms, booster clubs are the entrepreneurial agents of corporate athleticism.

Politically, booster clubs reinforce localism—their actions link alumni support and identity to state-supported public universities. The following statement expresses the ideological essence of boosterism at Clemson University.

> The mentality here is that ethics aren't as important as winning. The football team went 21–1 over the past two years and cheated like crazy; the basketall team has been 20–34 and is completely clean. Yet the boosters brag about the football program.[13]

The traditional relationship between winning and individual material reward for athletes will doubtless continue. Though the NCAA enforcement division employs ten full-time investigators and twenty-five part-time former FBI agents, NCAA rules have as yet not effectively checked booster clubs. On the contrary, table 6–1 indicates the sanctions meted out to institutions were mostly for providing illegal gifts to athletes. However, illegal payments as well as reports of numerous recruiting violations have received more media attention in recent years, thus magnifying the adverse political effects of such scandals on universities. Both the lucrative cash or in-kind stipends to students and the enthusiastic behavior of alumni have contributed to the pressures for more stringent administrative control of athletic programs.

## The Rhetoric of Administrative Reform— The 1983 NCAA Meeting

At the January 1983 meeting of the NCAA in San Diego, the delegates debated the need for new rules, and two themes dominated the political discourse.[14] The first theme had to do with the role of boosters, with many delegates contending that present practices of many Division I university boosters were out of control. This assertion inplied that the NCAA's rules for regulating athletic recruitment were ineffective. The second theme involved recruitment with delegates asserting that many students recruited to athletic programs lacked the requisite academic skills to matriculate as successful college students. An important element in this debate was the argument that if alumni behavior and student academic skills could be strengthened, the long-term interest of student-athletes would be well served. Adopting the measures on student recruitment would require student-athletes at Division I schools to meet higher academic standards so that they would enter college better prepared to perform as normal college students. More specifically, the supporters of recruitment reforms argued that academic standards would be improved if high school student-athletes possessed a combined verbal and mathematical Scholastic Aptitude Test (SAT) score of at least 700. Student-athletes would also be required to attain an average grade of C or better in a core high school curriculum. If these conditions held, student-athletes would be eligible as freshmen to engage in intercollegiate sports and more athletes would be students in an intellectually meaningful sense.

Basically, the recruitment reforms affirm that universities and student-athletes would be better off if student-athletes entered college with higher SAT scores. Universities, according to this analysis, would be better off because the "adoption of this proposal not only will restore credibility to our academic admissions, but also could restore meaning and integrity to a high school diploma."[15] In operational terms, the reforms maintain that the NCAA regulatory structures, through the strengthened sanctions and penalties on coaches, students, and boosters, would be able to limit sports commercialism. Normatively, the new recruitment rules assert the primacy of academic values as an eligibility criterion for all students, including athletes.

In spite of its forward-looking elements, the reforms can be technically criticized on several grounds. The *New York Times* reported in 1983 that only 36 of the top 116 National Basketball Association draftees earned college degrees, while 80 failed to do so.[16] Yet, no one argued at the NCAA convention that athletes with SAT scores of 700 would necessarily be more likely to attain a college degree. Even with higher SAT scores, it remains unclear whether more student-athletes would graduate from college. Nevertheless, the revised NCAA eligibility rules may make it easier for freshmen students to attain good standing as students when the regulations take effect in August 1986. But as the College Board has emphasized, SAT scores were never intended to be the sole criterion for admission to universities, nor were they even intended to be applied as a single admission standard for *all* universities. On these grounds, some contend that the NCAA SAT requirement and specified high school grade average constitute de facto national freshman eligibility criteria, and, as such, cannot be fairly applied to all Division I universities. American colleges and universities vary substantially in their student selection or recruitment criteria. Some universities require, in fact, less stringent recruitment standards than those adopted by the NCAA. In effect, the reform certainly violates the self-regulating, institutional pluralism of higher education.

Some NCAA delegates also argued that the new recruitment standards would yield a dissimilar effect for black athletes and for historically black colleges. However worthy the objectives of Proposition 48, some black educators at the convention claimed that access to educational opportunities would decline for many low-income youths, whose combined SAT scores fall well below the national average. Changes in educational standards should be left to individual universities. Some college presidents also argued that the new recruitment criteria should not depend on unreliable scholastic aptitude tests. Such tests would, it was argued, unfairly penalize those from low-income families, and the new proposition could not be applied equally to institutions unequal in their class and racial constituencies and educational mission. The basic point was that Proposition 48 would have unequal distributional consequences for many black, low-income athletes and for predominantly black colleges and universities. College Board figures (table 6–3) show that the average combined SAT scores for black students in 1982 barely exceeded 700.[17] Accordingly, the many students whose scores fell below the 700 mark would be ineligible to participate in intercollegiate sports during their freshman year. In short, some black educators believe that the autonomy, pluralism, and access to higher education should be maintained and that Proposition 48 would impinge on institutional standards.

The discourse on Proposition 48 reveals the extent to which commercialization in intercollegiate sports has taken hold in American universities. University officials scarcely argued at all that sports commercialization was antiethical to educational principles, as many educational studies had done in the past. Instead, the debates indicate the extent to which commercial sports was solidly accepted and institutionalized in higher education. Universities now have access to lucrative television contracts—a mechanism of corporate athleticism. Television payments provide considerable economic resources,

**Table 6–3**
**How Average SAT Scores Differ by Race**

|  | White Students | | | Black Students | | |
|---|---|---|---|---|---|---|
|  | *Verbal* | *Math* | *Total* | *Verbal* | *Math* | *Total* |
| 1976 | 451 | 493 | 944 | 332 | 354 | 686 |
| 1977 | 448 | 489 | 937 | 330 | 357 | 687 |
| 1978 | 446 | 485 | 931 | 332 | 354 | 686 |
| 1979 | 444 | 483 | 927 | 330 | 358 | 688 |
| 1980 | 442 | 482 | 924 | 330 | 360 | 690 |
| 1981 | 442 | 483 | 925 | 332 | 362 | 694 |
| 1982 | 444 | 483 | 927 | 341 | 366 | 707 |

Source: *The Chronicle of Higher Education,* January 26, 1983, p. 17.

thereby reinforcing the prestige associated with big-time athletic events like national or regional television appearances. Opponents of the new rules rightly point out that new regulations will reduce the access to education of low-income students, and yet, equally important, they seriously underestimate the ability of low-income students to measure up to higher academic standards. Certainly, the boundaries between opportunities and academic standards do not remain fixed and static; within limits, however, low-income students may yet respond positively to higher academic expectations.

Overall, then, the modified recruitment rules could help raise the academic preparation of high school athletes and thus should benefit future college student-athletes. Such rules provide one mechanism for integrating athletes into the general college student culture. Stronger academic preparation should in turn, weaken the ethos of athleticism—the student-athletes' perception that they, because they are "big men on campus," can approach their academic study indifferently. If student-athletes are treated as bona fide students, they may achieve higher grades. Many athletes are capable of reaching a higher academic standard. Whether as athletes or as students, those who study seriously will find themselves with career alternatives, either as professional athletes or in traditional occupational fields. On the other hand, the NCAA must reformulate the new rules so that they can be flexibly implemented at universities using varying admission criteria. The NCAA regulations, in short, cannot define a separate, higher, or more stringent standard for athletes than existing universities already set for regular students.

Seen in this context, Proposition 48 on student recruitment was not adopted simply to regulate the athletic recruitment process. It marked a step toward a *fundamental* transformation or reassertion of the NCAA's authority. No longer can the NCAA function as an authority unto itself, it must in the future be less responsive to market forces. Despite the steady ascendancy of market forces in the 1980s, authority has shifted to some degree from the athletic coaches to the presidents as a collective entity within the NCAA. This shift in authority confirms the trend toward the redefinition of the university's relationships with external powers, particularly those associated with athleticism. Moreover, the ACE proposal affirms its tacit conclusion that the NCAA's structure, as presently constituted, can no longer sustain academic values. In retrospect, it now seems clear that as television contracts were incorporated into college sports, presidential control over athletic activities steadily weakened; as booster clubs became more active, the presidents of individual universities faced greater resistance from athletic interests; and more recently, the belated political effort of university presidents to contain the NCAA, via a collective, off-campus presidential board, was defeated at the seventy-eighth NCAA conference.

Publicly, the presidents have asserted the primary of academic values. In doing so, they have exposed the corporate athletic system to public censure and helped mobilize the unorganized sports constituencies against the sports complex. With respect to athleticism, Glynn comments:

> These are the same values that dominate decisions of professional franchises and leagues. These are the same values dominating decisions of networks competing for broadcast rights to professional and collegiate sports and subsequently for viewing audiences. These are *the same values that dominate decisions or corporations* purchasing advertisements at rates determined by audience size. It is all one large national business and entertainment system that has a life of its own.[18]

Proposition 35 sought to institutionalize the boundaries between the competitive athletic programs of colleges and "intercollegiate athletics as an integral part of the educational system," thereby implying that the individual presidents at each campus cannot control the commercial dynamic in the college sports system. While a strong president might contain the athletic program on one campus, other presidents with different philosophies might support the business approach to sports on their campuses, thereby instilling new life into corporate athleticism as a *national* sports business ethos. If local business interests exert sufficient political pressures, and they do, many presidents would hire the coach who promised to take the college team to a conference championship. In effect, local business interests possess variable influence bases in different locales, making it extremely difficult for individual university presidents to maintain well-defined boundaries between college athletics and professional sports.

A similar set of political interests inhibits the NCAA's ability to regulate relations between universities and national television networks. Universities have different political interests and abilities to compete for such markets. The NCAA, for its part, possesses neither the legal authority nor the administrative power to contain the interests of specific universities. It was founded as a loosely structured association to control, monitor, and standardize rules pertaining to intercollegiate sports; it was not established to regulate contractual relationships between universities and national television networks. Accordingly, some universities have taken legal steps to bypass the restrictive regulations of the NCAA. Because these universities were successful, they have broken the NCAA's monopoly over television rights in football. At the more prestigious sports programs, athletic directors are now able to circumvent the NCAA's defunct regulations regarding television appearances in much the same way as they were able previously to circumvent academic norms associated with traditional university admissions requirements.

A final note. Almost without fanfare the NCAA, at it's January 1985 convention, gave the big-time Division I-A football powers what they have been wanting for for the last several years: increased autonomy and the ability to set their own rules "in matters relating to football."[19] The straw that undoubtedly broke the proverbial camel's back in this case probably was the threat of the big athletic powers to leave the NCAA because "too much control over their athletic programs" by smaller institutions, institutions that do not show the same problem or have the same market appeal.[20]

Not everyone thought this was good for the NCAA or good for intercollegiate athletics. John L. Toner, the ex-president of the NCAA, not unexpectedly felt that the move would cause "chaos." It seems at this sitting in late June 1985 that the NCAA is not faced with chaos. Rather, what we are witnessing is an organization desperately trying to retain vestiges of regulatory control and respect as its effectiveness is being reduced to a shell of its former self by the mounting forces of more powerful commercial and corporate actors. If present trends noted in this analysis continue, the NCAA, in a relatively short time, will be all but totally ignored as an effective force in the regulation of college sports.

## Declining Influence of the NCAA As Regulators

Several important observations can be drawn from this analysis. The influence of the NCAA as a regulatory agency seems largely marginal. Many schools, such as Wichita State and the University of San Francisco, for example, are repeatedly sanctioned by the NCAA, yet such sanctions have not altered certain illegal sports practices.[21] In many instances, institutions placed on probation can adapt to NCAA sanctions. Athletic programs at the University of Southern California or at the University of Oklahoma, for example, are unlikely to be adversely affected in the long run by NCAA sanctions, because given their powerfully institutionalized sports traditions, these schools will continue to attract exceptional athletes. Consequently, NCAA sanctions apparently are relatively ineffective when applied to the football or basketball powers. In cases like these, NCAA sanctions probably yield only marginal effects.

Because of the mainly symbolic nature of the NCAA sanctions, the existing sports hierarchy remains intact. Strong sports powers with well-developed sports traditions and facilities are less easily regulated. If sanctioned by the NCAA, some universities can compensate for a reduction in athletic scholarships by mobilizing alumni or others to gain resources. In other words, the actual costs of NCAA rule violations vary and sometimes are relatively low. By contrast, the universities with weaker, less-developed sports traditions are more likely to be strongly affected by NCAA regulations. Universities seeking to improve their national athletic rank may also be greatly affected by NCAA sanctions. Marginal sports programs may actually be more inclined than major programs to use material incentives to attract athletes of exceptional potential, so, whether NCAA sanctions actually function as punishment depends on existing conditions at the universities being sanctioned. Obviously, many broad assumptions about the effects of punishment in changing institutional behavior simply do not hold in all cases.[22]

Although NCAA regulations may be less effective than some observers assume, the association does perform important functions; its regulatory efforts are not entirely symbolic. NCAA regulations influence the public perception that college sports retain important features of amateurism. Equally important, NCAA sanctions against specific institutions reinforce public beliefs that college sports can sustain values of fairness, honesty, and discipline. Moreover, the NCAA regulations probably do reduce the number of blatant rule infractions at some universities. NCAA regulatory functions, however, may be effective in regulating the average, less prominent schools that participate in NCAA sponsored activities and championships. If the NCAA did not exist, intercollegiate sports would function in a quasi-anarchistic way. Market values, now to some degree checked, would dominate competitive sports. Under market arrangements, criteria such as the ability of each university to capture television markets through direct negotiations with television networks would control college athletics.

The Georgia-Oklahoma case against the NCAA impinges on the basic authority of the NCAA. If, for example, the NCAA is not able to regulate access to television receipts, its authority to impose administrative sanctions against institutions for violating NCAA rules may decline somewhat. In the present arrangement, the NCAA distributes resources garnered from television networks to member institutions. With the introduction of cable television, new sports markets are being created in many regions, but rather than permit the NCAA to negotiate on their behalf, some universities prefer to bargain directly with television interests. Such universities would no longer be required to distribute whatever television resources they obtain according to NCAA rules.

# Two Theories of Power

The tacit assumptions behind NCAA Proposal 35 and 36 rest on the two conflicting theories of power in the American university. Proposal 35 in seeking to create a presidential council with veto power implies that athletic directors, through support offered by athletic interests external to the university, have concentrated de facto power sufficient to control decision making in college athletics. This horizontal, special-interest group coalition exerts varying degrees of political influence on college sports issues, and hence, the regulation of these interests can appropriately be brought before the NCAA. Given the national scope of the political interests, the influence of this sports constituency cannot be regulated at only one university and cannot be regulated according to strict hierarchical control. In other words, athletic interest groups cannot be easily regulated through individual universities, mainly because sports interests are not entirely confined to the university. On the contrary, they are externally linked to market and to political forces in the larger society.

In essence, this argument parallels our claim that the organization of college sports is dominated by corporate values. We have argued that athletic departments, with the complicity of some university presidents, have institutionalized a set of values that support the organization of sports as a commercial, business enterprise. Although the presidents argue that this commercial structure is incompatible with academic values and that sports activity must be subordinate to academic values, we argue that corporate athleticism as it has evolved does not seem incompatible with the academic values of higher education, even though the corporate athletic complex, as presently organized, reduces the scope of presidential control in some instances. The growth of corporate sports is not an inevitable process, however. Indeed, despite presidential protestations about academic standards, university presidents in many instances have delegated authority to powerful booster interests. In the 1960s and early 1970s, many administrators granted substantial authority to semiautonomous athletic programs, thereby allowing well-organized boosters to seize political influence and to control substantially the direction of athletic programs. In this systemic context, the university quickly adapted to corporate sports. University presidents accepted the entrepreneurial process associated with corporate sports. At large, public universities, administrators found that a winning sports tradition helps to integrate heterogeneous academic and alumni constituencies. It similarly provides an activity that the public can identify with the university. In return, presidents capitalize on sports to generate social, political, and financial support for important university programs.

Similarly, the NCAA adapted to advancing corporate athleticism without seeming to realize the full implications of integrating college sports into television markets. The NCAA retained the symbolic vestiges of amateurism, and the norms of amateurism, accordingly, helped legitimize the transformation of college sports far beyond its amateur foundations. Although some coaches may not have felt comfortable with some of the rule changes, the substantive actions of the NCAA were highly pragmatic, thereby assisting the move to corporate sports. A whole series of NCAA actions—redshirting, more competitive recruiting, more athletic scholarships, weak enforcement procedures, the passage of freshman eligibility, and the acceptable of lax academic standards for athletes—all helped university sports programs to give greater scope to dynamic market forces. In effect, NCAA actions created the basis for the gradual transformation of amateurism. Indeed, they permitted university sports programs to upgrade and enlarge their athletic recruitment base, unleashing in the process new competitive forces in intercollegiate sports.

## The NCAA—Authority and Reform

In recent years, the NCAA has confronted multiple challenges to its authority. These crises have arisen in part because the NCAA positively responded to demands to present college sports on television, and in this way, the NCAA was an important mechanism for the structuring of athletic presentations on national television networks. The relaxation of recruitment rules and the expansion of the NCAA basketball national championship and the bowl games greatly facilitated the development of corporate athleticism. As Nebraska reminded everyone in the final minutes of the 1984 Orange Bowl, sports champions are winners; and athleticism as a cultural norm of mass society grows out of strong emphasis on decisive outcomes. In a highly complex society, sports is one social domain in which conflict can produce closure—real winners and losers, not just compromise.[23] The joys, pride, and special privileges associated with winning have deep roots in American society.[24]

The NCAA has presided over the advent of television into intercollegiate athletics, but it has not effectively maintained the boundaries between athletics and academic values. In a real sense, the NCAA's regulatory flexibility eventually fostered political conflict with universities and presidential authority. The NCAA also has not developed an adminstrative staff to regulate the more complex sports practices associated with big-time athletics, a staff capable of coping with the NCAA's regulatory responsibilities. More important, perhaps, the NCAA has not formulated a value system, centered on moral, academic, or amateur values, that can confront the expansive, competitive impulses associated with corporate market values. In sports, as elsewhere, the market simply erodes the traditional order, and faced with such forces, the NCAA failed to develop enforcement procedures or to allocate the resources necessary to make its own regulatory procedures operate effectively.

On the whole, the NCAA's response to market forces has been functionally adaptive. Its behavior over the past decade indicates a merely superficial concern with the conflicts between the amateur and the corporate concepts of athletics. Its procedures basically assumed that the student-athlete was a legitimate student, regardless of the scandalous evidence to the contrary. The persistent violations of NCAA recruiting regulations at specific schools clearly indicate that NCAA sanctions, even when applied, hardly exerted a sustained influence on recruitment behavior. It also seems clear that college sports as a system is far removed from the concept of amateurism embedded in the NCAA's constitution; a strikingly new system has come into being. In response to such changes, the NCAA was largely accommodationist: it created the political framework in which new interests, actors, and values could find scope at the expense of amateur conceptions of sports. In effect, the NCAA enabled universities to integrate college sports into a new system of cultural production and mass entertainment by helping them to amass financial resources and to distribute such resources among NCAA member institutions.

In the past two years, the assertion of presidential authority has brought about reforms in the NCAA. Reform proposals have reintroduced stronger academic criteria into the recruitment process to eliminate freshman eligibility and to add more stringent academic progress requirements. These reforms were adopted in 1982 as national standards for athletic recruitment, though American education has yet to adopt a national education policy. The most recent reform proposals, now rejected, would have instituted a forty-four-member presidential council with the authority to veto actions of the NCAA convention. Although the presidents mobilized politically on the issue of academic values, the idea of a strong presidential council was defeated. Based on the assumption that the NCAA in its present form is unable to regulate college sports, the proposal would have permitted the forty-four-member presidential council to function politically as a sort of Supreme Court, whose decisions could not be overruled and would be binding on all NCAA member institutions.

The defeat of Proposition 35 means that presidential authority is advisory, not mandatory. Ideologically, the approval of Proposition 36 suggests that the de facto control of the NCAA organization now remains for the time being with the athletic establishment. The principles of one-man-one-vote, decentralized norms for the regulation of college athletics, and the autonomy of the NCAA as an independent association are all affirmed with the passage of the advisory presidential council. The ACE sought to soften its proposals for bargaining purposes, but nevertheless it was unable to obtain the necessary support at the NCAA convention to secure the adoption of those proposals, even though these proposals would simply reinforce the boundaries between sports and academic values.

The NCAA, even when reformed, may possess neither the legitimacy nor the technical resources to check the influence of market criteria in the allocation of sports resources. Since the ability of universities to attract television resources depends on their value to the entertainment market, the allocation of financial resources will cluster around institutions with more developed sports programs; in time, this process will produce an unequal distribution of television resources, and if ineffectively regulated, the media-market mechanism will even displace the NCAA's formal criteria for allocating resources. This issue is recognized in the NCAA reform panel's conclusion that "the bonding together of institutions in order to generate maximum revenues is desirable, and that the distribution of income in athletics should mutually benefit the institutions involved and intercollegiate sports in general."[25] But the NCAA may not possess sufficient power to control the contractual behavior of individual universities, and under such circumstances, the influence of the NCAA and the less-powerful institutions will probably decline. The major contributors to the NCAA's weakness would be the big sports powers, as was tacitly recognized in the proposal for a presidential board to oversee NCAA regulations.

For the first time, the 1983 NCAA convention, the issue of who runs college sports was seriously raised. Television backed by the huge revenues it generates, wields ever greater power. Television commentators, discussing the convention vote, noted that the Nebraska-Penn State game was played on August 29th, 1984; college sports now seems to operate on a television cycle, not seasonally. For playing that game, Nebraska received $800,000, and for playing in the Orange Bowl, it received $1 million. At the end of the season, Mike Rozier, a star Nebraska halfback, signed a $3 million contract to play in the professional United States Football League, and partly because of such examples, 41,000 American youths now play college football. Only 1 percent of them will be drafted, and fewer still will stay in professional football. Approximately 14,000 college students play basketball; 280 of them will be drafted in the professional basketball league, but only 50 will stay. In other words, large numbers of athletes readily respond to the powerful financial incentives associated with college sports in an effort to gain the fame and fortune that awaits the professional athlete. Whatever the effects of the NCAA reform recommendations, it seems unlikely that the reforms will fully control the dollars, pressures, or differential academic standards associated with corporate athleticism.

In addition to the NCAA reforms, university presidents have wrought some measure of change in the NCAA's regulatory context. Presidential leadership in the NCAA has effected some important normative changes. For instance, more universities have added academic advisors to their corporate athletic infrastructure; Rutgers University, for example, appointed in 1983 an athletic academic advisor shortly after the 1982 NCAA vote on student recruitment and academic standards. Because of the financial incentives, athletes in high school and college will no doubt, try to improve their academic performance, in order to meet the eligibility requirements for participation in college-level sports. They have powerful incentives to do so, for the incentives associated with big-time sports, as the president of Rice University recently declared, affect institutions as well as individuals.

Despite the defeat of the strong reform proposal, the NCAA should henceforth perform more effectively as a regulatory agent. Indeed, it recently increased its administrative enforcement budget for 1982–83 significantly, making that function a separate budget item so that the actual administrative enforcement process can be monitored in terms of performance outcomes.

Nevertheless, some schools will continue to reap major benefits from corporate athleticism. New regulatory procedures, for example, cannot eliminate natural inequalities that provide a few universities with exceptional market positions because of their talent pools, climate, and large populations. Access to these resources is directly related to location: universities in California, Texas, Pennsylvania, and Florida should continue to dominate college football.

## The Growing Power of Corporate Athleticism

On June 27, 1984, the Supreme court in a 7–2 decision ended more than thirty years of NCAA control of college football by ruling in favor of the Georgia-Oklahoma challenge to the NCAA's right to limit the number of college games telecast and to prevent universities from directly negotiating contracts with major cable and national television networks. The Court ruled that NCAA regulations were "inconsistent" with antitrust laws, contending that such regulations restrict the "importance of consumer preference." In this way, the Court terminated the NCAA's right to regulate the role of television in intercollegiate sports. The ruling marked the legal triumph of corporate athleticism, for the NCAA should henceforth find it more difficult to preserve even the fading ethos of amateurism. As a result of the Court's decision, the NCAA can no longer exercise such unreasonable constraints on trade as (1) setting the price for particular football telecasts; (2) securing "exclusive network contracts" tantamount to a group boycott of other potential broadcasters, with a threat of sanctions against its own members or a threatened boycott of potential broadcast competitors; and (3) placing artificial limits on the production of televised college football. Both the challenge to the NCAA's authority and the supreme Court's decision were formulated strictly in terms of market norms.

In his dissenting opinion, Justice White emphasized that the NCAA member institutions had conceived their "competitive athletic programs to be a vital part of the educational system, rather than . . . as a purely commercial venture in which colleges and universities participate solely, or even primarily, in the pursuit of profits." He noted further that the NCAA sought to "provide a public good—a viable system of amateur athletics—that most likely would not be provided in a perfectly competitive market." While the majority opinion of the Court recognized the "critical" role the NCAA played in "the maintenance of a revered tradition of amateurism in college sports," the majority found this role could not justify the NCAA's use of market power to introduce a "naked restraint on price and output" with respect to television entertainment and appearances. Clearly, the Court has legitimized the central role of market forces in the presentation of college football. The universities and conferences with stronger, more commercial athletic traditions can freely negotiate with television networks, and one commentator asserted that the Court's ruling "will perpetuate the strong getting stronger and the weak [being] eliminated altogether from the network television plan."[26]

The market position of the dominant football powers grows stronger in numerous ways: enrollment, recruitment advantages, and financial rewards will gradually shift to those schools that appear most frequently on television. In a more complete corporate system, television networks generate larger markets and audiences, which suggests therefore that the corporate athletic power of some universities may significantly increase in a deregulated sports market. Perhaps offsetting the potential power of strong athletic programs, however, is the spread of athletic talent to many universities as a result of more intensive recruitment and training procedures. The market will not sustain the relative equality between the rich and the poor schools, which was one of the modest benefits of NCAA regulatory control, such as it was—yet in a relatively open sports market, the role of competitive forces should grow. In time, the established sports powers should recieve smaller television receipts for each television appearance but will probably have more games televised.

Placed in broad perspective, sports administration has taken on new dimensions. In the 1980s, the NCAA was the focus of conflict over reform efforts as new rules and procedures to regulate intercollegiate athletics were put in place. In its modified administrative framework, NCAA sanctions are now broader in scope: students and coaches are subject to sanctions and more stringent standard of behavior. Equally important, the decision-making procedures of the NCAA have been strengthened, giving added weight to adacemic interests through the collective authority of the president's council. In view of these changes, corporate athletics must now operate within more-tightly structured administrative boundaries.

Through the president's council, university presidents possess a substantial capacity to control their sports programs. Consequently, the discrepancy between the university's goals and those of the athletic complex should be reduced. Because they are more closely monitored, sports programs should be better managed and thus avoid the scandal and corruption associated with aggressive commercial sports. Though the NCAA reforms may reduce athleticism, they do not appear to herald the restoration of amateurism in college sports, for the Supreme Court's 1984 decision to recognize the role of market forces in college sports seems to imply that full control of the corporate sports system may lie beyond the NCAA's formal administrative reach.

The unanswered question, of course, is how much the Court's recognition of college sports as a commercial activity will adversely constrain the NCAA's regulatory role. Clearly, more college games will appear on national and regional television networks but many schools, except for universities with winning traditions, will receive less television money. In addition, college sports on television will continue to provide exciting mass entertainment. As local neighborhoods decline, people move to new locales and regions, and individuals become isolated from familiar social groupings, more leisure time becomes available, and watching sports on television is an enjoyable way to "fill" such leisure. Because the sports television market and the administration of college sports have developed beyond and moved away from the American university, additional procedures will eventually be needed to regulate college sports. To the excent that American society changes and the sports market evolves, the NCAA will continue to face troublesome regulatory issues arising from the more complex structure of college sports. Despite the strengthening of the NCAA in recent years, it would accordingly be premature to say at this point that university presidents have discovered an effective way to contain the relentless commercialization of college sports.

## Notes

1. David Nelson, "Governance of Intercollegiate Athletics—Who Is Running the Asylum?" (Paper presented to the Conference on Sports and Higher Education, Skidmore College, 18 March 1983).

2. See *New York Times.*

3. *Quoted in Otis A. Singletary, "Getting Presidents More Involved in College Sports," New York Times,* 8 January 1984, sec. S, p. 2.

4. For the formation of these questions, see David W. Welborn, *Governance of Federal Regulatory Agencies* (Knoxville, Tenn.: University of Tennessee Press, 1977), pp. 3–13; see also Gordon S. White, Jr., "NCAA Overseer Proposed," *New York Times,* 16 December 1983, sex. B, p. 7.

5. White, "NCAA Overseer Proposed," sec. B, p. 7.

6. David P. Gardner, (president of the University of Utah and chairman of the Committee), cited in *Chronicle of Higher Education,* 13 October 1982, p. 17.

7. See the 1929 Savage Report on the dangers of commercialism.

8. See Edward T. Foote, Comments in *Chronicle of Higher Education,* 23 January 1985, p. 31.

9. See Gregory S. Sojka, "The Evolution of the Student-Athlete in America: From the Divinity to the Devine" (Paper presented at the Conference on Sports and Higher Education, Skidmore College, March 1982), 2.

10. See Kenneth Denlinger and Leonard Shapiro, *Athletes for Sale* (New York: Thomas Y. Crowell, 1975), 214–215; and Lesley Visser, "College Boosters: Out of Control?" *Boston Globe,* 3 July 1983.

11. See N. Scott Vance, "3 Institutions Find Athletes' Grades Low: Mixed Results in Big 10 University Study," *The Chronicle of Higher Education,* May 11, pp. 7–8.

12. Ibid.

13. See Leslie Visser, "College Boosters," 39.

14. See National Collegiate Athletic Association, *1983 Convention Proceedings,* 77th Annual Meeting, 10–12 Jan. 1983, San Diego, Calif.

15. Ibid., 107.

16. See N. Scott Vance, "Two-Thirds of Basketball Stars Drafted by Pros have yet to Graduate from College," *Chronicle of Higher Education,* July 6, 1983, pp. 13–14.

17. See Huel D. Perkins, "Higher Academic Standards for Athletes Do not Discriminate against Blacks," *The Chronicle of Higher Education,* September 7, 1985, p. 88 on the need for black athletes to commit themselves to higher academic standards as part of their reason for attending institutions of higher education.

18. Rev. Edward Glynn, cited in Singletary, "Getting Presidents More Involved," sec. S, p. 2.

19. Charles S. Farrell, "NCAA Votes to Give Some Autonomy to Major Football-Playing Institutions," *The Chronicle of Higher Education* January 23, 1985, p. 31.

20. Ibid.

21. The experience of the University of San Fransisco illustrates how difficult it may be for even a conscious university administration to control basketball program. After repeated violations of NCAA rules, the university eliminated and then restored and restructured its basketball program. See the Rev John Lo Schiavo, "Restoring, and Controlling, a College Sport," Section 5, *New York Times,* C/W p. 2.

22. See Denlinger and Shapiro, *Athletes for Sale,* 214–215.

23. For the formulation of these questions, see Welborn, *Governance of Federal Regulatory Agencies,* 3–13; and White, "N.C.A.A. Overseer Proposed," sec. B, p. 7.

24. See the Miller *Lite Report,* p. 50.

25. See Recommendations from NCAA's Special Panel on Problems in College Athletics," *The Chronicle of Higher Education,* November 9, 1983 p. 29.

26. Cited in Peter W. Kaplan, "Rush Likely to Sign Up More Games," *New York Times,* June 28, 1984, B8–9.

# 7

# Whither the New Sports System: Proposals for Reform

Nearly all serious discussions of college athletics include proposals for restructuring some dimension of sports.[1] Such proposals usually try to rationalize the existing system by bringing it closer in line with an idealized amateur conception of college sports, or, alternatively, reform proposals may seek to reduce illegal practices. For these reasons, heightened media attention to recent scandals has spurred numerous reforms or induced college presidents to devote more careful administrative attention to college sports. At the same time, however, increased recognition now exists that college coaches are paid to win; losing coaches are fired, while winning coaches receive more substantial pecuniary rewards. So at best, then, the incentives for reforming college sports are contradictory, and ultimately, the incentives for substantial reforms seem relatively weak. In this chapter, we examine three possible directions of future reform efforts, noting the institutional and political constraints on each reform option.

## The Semiprofessional Option: Further Commercialization

One way to reorganize college sports would be to make them semiprofessional.[2] In some respects, college sports might be organized like the baseball farm system. College athletes would be paid modestly for services rendered and would also participate in long-term programs of skill development prior to their movement into the professional hierarchy. This proposal recognizes that college sports, including college baseball, are a primary training ground for aspiring professional athletes. More and more, university sports programs are displacing the traditional farm system still used in baseball, particularly as educational requirements in American society continue their upward movement. Like professional training, sports requires increasingly long periods of certification, and the universities are well-placed to award such certification, in sports as in education.[3] College sports, in this view, may constitute a new method of professional sports training, one compatible in many fundamental ways with the ongoing commercialization of leisure in late industrial society.

In this scheme, athletes would not necessarily enter academic programs. Indeed, some would argue that, properly organized, college sports should be separated from the university, inasmuch as such sports have already outgrown their amateur foundations. Or, alternatively, if universities continue as the site for semiprofessional sports, such activities might be administered by a separate university corporation. College sports as a semiprofessional, commercial activity would then merely retain symbolic links to universities and colleges. College students might also continue to participate in semiprofessional sports, but they would be paid, and college attendance would not be the sole or exclusive channel for recruiting athletes.

In a semiprofessional system, athletes would be recruited widely, strictly according to their talent, regardless of whether or not they attend college. Unlike the present system, the semiprofessional system would be open to all highly skilled athletes who could then gain access to the training needed to develop their exceptional talents. Further, coaches would be hired on the basis of their won/lost records, without regard to their formal academic credentials; they would be sports managers, colorful and eccentric, no doubt, and perhaps no longer role models in the traditional sense. In this system, sports would change in response to consumer demands, and over the long term, the semiprofessional sports would evolve, separating gradually from amateur sports and from the university.

This reform would produce a commercially viable semiprofessional college sports system, but remnants of the current college sports system would persist. Colleges might retain minor sports and could offer a broad array of intramural sports. Because they are truly an amateur sports system, intramural sports might receive greater priority in university athletics. Under this arrangement, the values of amateurism would be reinstituted for the university community and transferred to intramural sports, which might then be accorded enhanced institutional prestige as well as additional financial resources.

Ultimately, the proposal for making college sports semiprofessional rests on powerful economic realities, but the reform of college sports along these lines would encounter substantial political resistance. Universities seeking to institute a formal semiprofessional system would risk losing the political support of legislatures, local businesses, alumni, the general public, and student constituencies. Although the concept of amateurism no longer plays any real part in college athletics, the public retains a strong symbolic attachment to the idea of games unadulterated by raw commercial values. In other words, the idea of amateurism perpetuates a residual symbolic attachment between athletes and spectators inasmuch as it softens the commercial edges of college sports.

## Residual Amateurism: The Retention of Traditional Values

A second way of reorganizing college sports involves the restoration of amateurism, or what we term *residual amateurism.*[4] In this scheme, academic values are consistently given high priority. The athlete is recruited primarily because of his athletic skills, but also because he can meet established academic standards. Corporate athleticism is present, however, exerting subtle pressures on the university's effort to sustain traditional academic values. University officials may periodically reiterate the institution's commitment to college sports, but academic values clearly constitute the central core of the university's historic identity. Even at these institutions, however, the imperatives of winning will remain important: a losing coach will still be fired, and student and alumni pressures must be satisfied at least in some measure.

In this system, presidential leadership would be periodically asserted to place the university's sports system solidly within the university's broad educational mission. Colleges would retain the so-called minor sports, which would be supplemented by intramural sports.

Currently at many private elite universities, for example, faculty leadership remains strong. Bolstered by substantial academic authority, faculty members at these institutions serve attentively on oversight committees to ensure that academic standards are closely adhered to in university sports programs. Because academic values are vigorously affirmed at these institutions, faculty members of oversight committees exercise genuine authority in helping to maintain clear boundaries between academic and athletic values. Simply put, academic values are consistently supported and reinforced at certain first-rank private universities.

By contrast, at many large, public universities during the 1960s and 1970s, faculty authority waned. Faculty at these universities retreated from university governance, thus providing many university administrators with the political space to adopt measures advancing the centralization process. Just as greater presidential assertion at elite universities may facilitate the restoration of firm academic control over athletics, the rise of specialized public managers at other universities indicates a significant trend in another direction, toward general corporate management of the American university. The route to administrative reform may vary according to the type of university. Nevertheless, athletic directors at large, public universities should eventually feel the full effect of this evolving trend.

Effective administrative oversight in the residual amateur model is also facilitated when students and alumni are regularly consulted on important academic decisions. This active involvement in sports administration would occur even when students and alumni exercise no formal role in key decisions. Sometimes, alumni may be asked to extend financial support to athletic programs when universities seek capital to build additional sports facilities but in this scheme, the alumni would be isolated from the actual management of resources for athletic programs. Boosters would also cease to intervene directly in the recruitment of athletes. In short, boosters in the residual amateur model would no longer link athletic programs to the market values of corporate athleticism. Residual amateurism, in these terms, appears most likely to prevail at institutions with strong academic traditions that have the power to sustain stable administrative controls at nearly every level of the university hierarchy.

A variant of residual amateurism, which we term the *restoration of amateurism* model, also exists at some universities. This strategy may come into play when a fully developed system of corporate sports breaks down. In this situation, restructuring the athletic program may lead to the restoration of the amateur system. On the basis of the analysis developed here, however, this restoration strategy must be regarded as unstable, even experimental, so great are the persisting market pressures.

The instability built into this strategy can be seen in the case of the University of San Francisco. Following repeated NCAA sanctions for violations and a scandal involving a prominent basketball player, the University of San Francisco at first dropped and then restructured its basketball program. Under the control of a Jesuit priest working as athletic director, San Francisco has hired a basketball coach presumably committed to an amateur philosophy, and the university's basketball program is now geared towards playing only in the West. The university's strong academic traditions broke down in the face of multiple pressures toward corporate athleticism, but this new policy might possibly take San Francisco out of that national corporate system.

On the assumption, as university President Lo Schiavo put it, that "if it has been done, it can be done," amateur norms are being restored at the University of San Francisco. Basketball players are recruited locally. Full scholarships are given. The university's mission in this case is to demonstrate that a basketball program can stay clean and still win. Accordingly, alumni at San Francisco help raise funds for sports programs, but reportedly are no longer involved in basketball recruiting. In the San Francisco case, NCAA violations, together with adverse publicity, were sufficiently powerful incentives to induce a profound restructuring of a corporate athletic program. A strong academic tradition seems to be the most important element in a vigorous reform strategy that seeks to restore amateurism.

Nevertheless, cases of amateurism, residual or restored, do not necessarily contradict our general argument that corporate athleticism is now the dominant tradition in college sports. For the most part, efforts to sustain variants of amateurism are essentially rearguard actions, and it is too soon to know whether such efforts can be sustained for long. A change in presidential leadership—or other factors—can quietly signal the final demise of amateurism, and in effect, the conditions that facilitate the adoption of amateur models are specific, even unique conditions. Neither residual amateurism nor restored amateurism at select universities are general reform models: the new college sports system has moved definitively beyond these options. The existence of these models at select universities merely confirm the still incomplete, evolving nature of the corporate sports system.

If, as our analysis implies, the sources of corruption in college sports are systemic in nature, viable reform proposals must likewise be systemic in scope. If one commercially oriented university is able to institute questionable sports practices, then others will follow, and the norms associated with corporate athleticism are likely to continue, for universities love athletic winners and winning serves multiple purposes for presidents, alumni, and boosters, as well as faculty and students. Reform proposals that fail to address the systemic dimensions of the new sports system cannot hope to reduce pressure towards corporate athleticism.

At this writing a special NCAA convention called by the newly created 44-member Presidents' Commission has concluded its business and agreed to mete out the strongest sanctions ever imposed against colleges and coaches who violate NCAA recruiting, academic, and ethical standards.[5]

The special meeting, only the fifth since the founding of the NCAA in 1906, was called to address the "integrity crisis" in college sports and was dominated by presidents and chancellors of Division I universities and colleges. Conspicuous by their absence were coaches and athletic directors of the major college sports programs. So much was this a Presidents' show that Donna Lopiano, the women's athletic director at the University of Texas was prompted to remark: "You don't argue during an invasion."[6]

Many of the 200 attending presidents called the meeting historic and a first step in making sure ". . . that athletic departments are under tight control of their colleges and that chronic rule breakers are severely penalized."[7] Whether the actions taken were indeed historical will depend on how effectively the reforms are implemented.

Nevertheless, what the presidents did was significant given the rash of NCAA recruiting and gambling violations that seem to appear weekly on sports pages across the country. Repeat offenders seemed to be the main target of the presidential "invasion." Thus, the new rules would: bar all intercollegiate competition for up to two years by the team involved in the more recent infraction at an institution that was penalized for a major infraction within the previous five years; prohibit coaches in that sport from coaching during that same period, even if they move to another institution; divide rule violations into two categories—major and secondary. Penalties for violations were strengthened. Each institution would be required to: conduct a self-study of its sports programs every five years as a condition of its membership; give the NCAA academic information about its entering freshman, its athletes' compliance with continuing eligibility requirements, and graduation rates; have external audits of all its athletic programs, including booster clubs.[8]

Whether these presidential reforms will do the trick is debateable. One thing is certain: athletic directors, coaches, and boosters will not sit still and watch a group of CEO's try to legitimize academic standards by ruining the athletic goose laying golden eggs.

A few head coaches, reacting to the "death penalty" (the nickname attached to the stern measures adopted by the presidents), are beginning to answer the presidents' invasion with volleys of their own. They cite the fact that hitting programs with these penalties will be tantamount to sending them to their graves, not to be seen again for two to three years, if at all. They also suggest that presidents don't want to cheat but want to win. The coaches seem to imply that one goes with the other, at least in big-time athletics. Barry Switzer drew a keen bead when he suggested that before any action is taken on the presidents' proposals people should consider ". . . the ramifications of shutting down a major football program"—one like his own with a $10 million budget.[9]

Citing a multiplier effect, Switzer went on to suggest that if football dies (that death penalty again), the effects would be catastrofic. Other sports, non–revenue-producing sports, will die as well. Not only will groundskeepers lose their jobs, but more importantly the financial community will be up in arms and sue the university because it is involved in bond issues for the building and expansion of stadiums.[10] Add to Switzer's list the wrath of powerful state legislators and governors who look forward to rubbing off some of the magic from a winning football or basketball team. We noted earlier that few if any schools can expect to win big without the support of highly developed booster organizations. We noted as well that boosters were, among other things, the main links with the business system. College sports is now inextricably intertwined with that system. No presidential proposals, however couched will alter this basic fact. As a result, they will, like so many reform proposals, fall short of the mark of preserving the "integrity" of intercollegiate athletics.

At the same time, many universities seek to redefine the managerial president's role in response to broad market forces, including corporations. Given the cultural hegemony of market norms in mass society, even in Clark Kerr's multiversity, this assertion of a new presidential bureaucracy in higher education will not be easy to implement, and yet, we believe that ultimately it will succeed. American universities crossed a momentous institutional threshold in the 1980s. Accordingly, they will in the 1980s be less insulated from a broad array of social forces. If correct, these analyses suggest that the multifunctional role of the American university is being enlarged, partly because the market introduces alternative principles of stratification into the university. A new system of stratification results from the connection between the university and sports markets: universities, as we argue, have internalized market criteria through the role specialization of the student-athlete and through the institutionalization of the corporate athletic infrastructure.

This functional stratification and specialization creates its own socialization process, as the athletes become more athletic commodities than students. Segregated dormitory living, athletic tutoring, training, and other specialized activities occur within the athletic infrastructure. In this way, the athlete exists primarily as a market agent, whose educational aspirations, if they exist, can be institutionally channeled—that is, politically structured— through the athletic programs at major universities.

But the universities' public agenda appears to be changing. More and more, universities must position themselves in relation to the business and government structures of American society. On the whole, however, they lack the means to do so. Yet, as one study notes, "It is often through new academic specialties and through athletics that the university seeking to rise in the academic hierarchy can most quickly and easily attract national attention."[11] In the 1980s universities seem more dependent on government funding for research in order to accelerate their contribution to high-tech industries. In the face of a rapidly changing national economy, sports help universities to position themselves politically in order to gain greater public financial support. The mark of a university "on the make" is a mad scramble for both football stars and professional luminaries,[12] for sports is one way that universities can reach out to mass publics.[13] To the extent that universities must appeal to the public for funds, then we can expect the performance of sports teams—the most publicly visible component of the university—to improve substantially. Unless the amateur option can deal with this larger issue—that is, the political quest for public support—it can hardly resolve the systemic pressures associated with corporate sports.

## The Maintenance of Corporate Athleticism

The third reform option asserts in essence that the existing sports system constitutes a structurally integrated system. It rejects the amateur model as incompatible with the commercial realities of contemporary college sports as a mass entertainment system and also argues that the semiprofessional model is equally incompatible with the political realities of the modern university. While all elements of the sports market are not yet fully integrated, the existing sports system is sufficiently developed that no major political interests in the new sports system seems willing to make substantial concessions or is willing to opt for alternative arrangements. Analysis should, nevertheless, explore the incentives that might influence the various actors in the sports system to accept reforms that leave the basic system intact, while moderating illegal or corrupt practices.

But since powerful incentives to political reform are largely absent, the most likely prospect is that the present sports system will slowly evolve. Rules will be modified in a piecemeal fashion, and modest efforts will be made periodically to preserve cherished symbols of amateurism. Major efforts, nevertheless, will also be made at times to rationalize corrupt behavior, since sports exercises such a powerful moral influence on American culture. At another level, sports will continue to be an important metaphor for modern social organization. Athletic performance will become more intensive and reach new heights of exceptional performance. In effect, present conditions in college sports constitute a stable reality since they integrate powerful institutional and political interests; small adjustments bringing the present system closer to shifting market realities can nevertheless be expected.

In the evolving sports context, many of the patterns noted in previous chapters will persist for reasons already described, but important changes in corporate athleticism seem likely to occur. The informal autonomy of sports programs will be enhanced: some sports programs may become legally separated from universities, while retaining important symbolic connections, such as the university's name. Such ad hoc adjustments will reflect the significant financial autonomy of well-developed athletic programs. Less prestigious athletic programs, of course, will remain institutionally connected to universities. College sports will also remain effectively tied to the entertainment market. Amateurism as a normative concept rested squarely in the university, whereas corporate athleticism is anchored deeply in the entertainment market. Hence, changes in that market effectively will influence the future evolution of college sports.

Corporate athleticism also represents an early phase of the university's unfolding relation to the market.[14] In this respect, the transformation of college sports merely exemplifies in specific terms the general change in the relationships between the university and external institutions, like government and business.[15] In the 1980s the university will forge a more extensive, multifaceted relationship to the business corporation. A recent Carnegie Foundation Report put the matter succinctly when it stated that as corporate political and economic power continues to rise, higher education will find itself negotiating less with government bureaucrats and more with the business community. The Report further pointed out what we have already stressed: "Increasingly, academic decisions are being shaped by decisions in corporate board rooms."[16] Corporate athleticism is a special element in this broader trend towards the closer integration of market forces into American society. Although the commercialization of sports has evolved new forms, on the historical evidence this commercialization process is not fundamentally incompatible with academic values.

Corporate athleticism is also the product of decisions informally manipulated by aggressive, commercially oriented athletic departments. Through the creation of public demand for college sports, scheduling of specific events, extension of the sports season, and definition of national sports markets, television provided the monetary incentive (by exerting a degree of control over the principal means) for the development (production) of corporate athleticism. In turn, decentralized administrative structures in universities offered little opposition and gave corporate athleticism a particularly fertile political (administrative) arena in which to develop. Without weak administrative hierarchies, corporate athleticism could not so easily have developed.

The type of organizational nexus within the university makes the adjustment to market demands relatively easy. Though some might argue that the university experience with athletics typically deviates from the norms of higher education, the uses of the university are varied, as Clark Kerr reminds us. In this perspective, the institutionalized political economy of sports is typical of numerous organizational forms nurtured within the university. That is, this case illustrates the kinds of pressures exerted by external markets and government agencies on the university to absorb a larger production and research role in American society. These pressures are not new. What is new is that the accumulating political factions within the university make it more difficult for university presidents to manage the diverse array of interests through traditional institutional means. The clientele clusters outside the university will yield alternative organizational structures in time, but the density of networks created by specialized, informal interest groups has brought about weak presidencies at most universities.

In this institutional setting, the systemic power of the athletic department grows in such a way that a coach is able to achieve the complex goal of producing a major, winning sports team. Such a coach builds his personal authority as a public official. By the same token, the successful athletic department is able to generate external resources in the form of additional support from the alumni or from the local business community. One could argue that sports have legitimized the commercialization process in the university. Political variables reinforce an economic resource-generating process, and through this process, the political economy restructures authority to a certain extent in the university, not according to hierarchical or presidential control, but around a politically defined functional autonomy and around economic motivations. In this process we see an interaction between the economic and political variables that constitute the functional anchors, as it were, of corporate athleticism. The character of these interactions—as was illustrated in media scandals—changed in the 1970s. In its focus on recruiting, drug scandals, and academic performance standards for athletes, the news media helped intensify efforts to reform college sports.

The institution of the sports market within the university is different in degree, not in kind. A comparable model can be seen in the research institutes of various kinds established within the university to serve the interests of governments and foundations. Typically, the directors of such institutions receive higher salaries, and the institutes provide faculty, rather than students, with financial benefits. Eventually, many such institutes spin off to become independent of the university. Sports commercialization, however, seems more deeply rooted in the university structure; it has been a persistent, ongoing trend within American universities for nearly forty years. Minimally influenced by academic considerations, the present sports system has coexisted with academic values without doing great harm to general academic standards, claims to the contrary notwithstanding.

In the maintenance model, the university can be characterized as facing conflicting tendencies: some aspects of its evolving reorganization restrain corporate athleticism, and at the same time others facilitate its consolidation. In reality, however, both trends reflect the development of a corporate university. Curricular changes, new disciplines, business funding for university research, the impending decline of the arts, social sciences, and humanities all indicate the universities' uneven integration during the 1980s into the national economy, in marked contrast to the free-floating period of student academic study in the 1960s. In this and in other respects, the organization of college sports parallels in the 1980s the general rise of corporate power in American society. In view of these integrative changes, universities may find it difficult to sustain distinct normative standards, such as those associated with amateurism.

Seen in these terms, corporate athleticism scarcely constitutes an institutional distortion of the American higher education; on the contrary, it is the culmination of commercial trends long present in the American university. The new student-athlete may represent an erosion of the traditional concept of the student, but seen through different lenses, he could equally well represent the new student, who approaches the university strictly as a narrow, individual consumer. He views learning, above all, through the lens of the marketplace. He enters a specific university solely because he was offered an enticing package. In this respect, the athlete is not at all the deviant nonstudent, but is truly the student of the future.

In view of the recent Supreme Court rulings, the maintenance of the existing college sports system in the present circumstances should translate into the further consolidation of corporate athleticism. Even so, modest reforms can occur, even assuming the continued presence of corporate athleticism. Like large corporations, for example, college sports will continue to internationalize it recruitment networks. In the future, more athletes will come from Europe, Latin America, Africa, and the Pacific, because as college sports function increasingly as markets, the incentives to widen recruitment networks must grow. The spread of rigorous training procedures and coaching methods will permit more such athletes to participate in American track, football, and basketball. Another potential reform might be to sanction athletes, not universities, for flagrantly violating NCAA regulations. Athletes accepting gifts, cars, money, or other remunerations would be ineligible to play sports for specific periods; these sanctions would punish athletes in ways they would take seriously, by restricting their opportunity to hone their skills in rigorous competition. Furthermore, such athletes would no longer have access to the media or the chance to raise their market price. Another area of reform might affect scholarships or other kinds of financial aid to athletes. Flexible scholarships could recognize the needs of athletes from low-income backgrounds; additional stipends might be given to students unable to work part-time because of legitimate commitments to the university.

## Conclusion

In these ways, carefully targeted reforms can encourage modest adjustments in sports organization and behavior to eliminate—or at least effectively contain—the most corrupt features of college sports. One weakness in any reform proposal is that enforcing new rules fully is difficult. In a highly competitive, corporate sports system, some coaches and players will, no doubt, always conceive incentives to violate the most precise regulations. Nevertheless, as we all know, that's the way a market operates: it follows its own bottom line, rewarding both honest and corrupt producers as long as they produce.

## Notes

1. We are indebted to Joel Rogers for his helpful critical comments on this chapter and on other parts of the manuscript.
2. The semiprofessional model was outlined in a paper presented by David Nelson at the Conference on Sports and Higher Education, Skidmore College, March 18, 1983.
3. For an interesting reform proposal, see Leonard Koppett, *Sports Illusion, Sports Reality* (Boston: Houghton Mifflin Company, 1981). Among other things, he proposes that the NCAA ensure that the graduation rates of athletes match the average annual graduation rates at particular institutions of higher education. He would therefore curtail the NCAA's regulatory role by concentrating on the output side, that is, on the production of college athletes in relation to institutional norms. His proposals fail to examine, however, the political and economic context of the NCAA's role and the dearth of political incentives for the reform of college education.
4. See A. Bartlett Giamatti, *The University and the Public Interest* (New York: Atheneum, 1981), 77–194. His chapter on "Yale and Athletics," is a forceful state-

ment of the role of amateurism at a major research university. We have drawn heavily on this chapter for a definition of the amateur position and the conflicts between amateurism and commercial tendencies in intercollegiate sports. Factual statements on San Francisco's restored basketball program were presented on the MacNeil-Lehrer Show.

5. Gordon S. White, Jr., "N.C.A.A. Sets Stiffer Penalties for Violations," New York Times, June 22, 1985, p. 1.

6. Ibid.

7. Charles S. Farrell, "NCAA Votes Tougher Rules, Penalties; 198 Presidents at Special Convention," *The Chronical of Higher Education,* July 3, 1985, p. 1.

8. Ibid.

9. *The Dominion Post,* June 30, 1985, p. 6-d.

10. Ibid.

11. Clark Kerr, *The Uses of the University.* Cambridge, Mass.: Harvard University Press, 1982, p. 90.

12. Ibid.

13. "Sports has become a central part of American culture, a metaphor for achievement and a tool of business." Jane Gross, "Companies Find Sports Good for Business," *New York Times,* see C, p. 1.

14. See Paul Starr, *The Social Transformation of American Medicine* (New York: Basic Books, 1982), particularly chap. 5, "The Coming of the Corporation," for an insightful analysis of parallel trends making for the rise of corporate medicine. Though we emphasize the rise of corporate sports within the university, other disciplines, fields, or departments within the university may also have strong corporate orientations, reflecting the degree of their involvement in market or government relations. On the growth of federal government sponsorship at one research university, see "Federally Sponsored Research at Harvard," *Harvard Gazette,* 4 December 1984, pp. 9–11. The report indicates the extensive growth in federally sponsored research at Harvard since World War II. While the report stresses Harvard's efforts to protect its corporate or academic interests, the report does not discuss the ways in which government contracts have influenced faculty relations, promotional criteria for professors, or changing standards of student teaching.

15. Despite vast improvements, trends within the university indirectly promote the creation of new external links between schools, departments, and external government and business agencies. See the analysis of the university president as executive officer or manager in Clark Kerr, "Presidential Leadership," *Change* (September 1984):32–36. Since the 1950s, Kerr notes, presidents have changed from academic leaders to "managers." Consequently, large segments of the university have become "self-policing" or have evolved in response to the availability of strong external financial resources and demands for technical research.

16. Carnegie Foundation for the Advancement of Teaching, *The Control of the Campus* (Washington, D.C.: 1982), 86.

# Bibliography

Adler, Richard, and Douglass Cater, eds., *Television as a Culture Force*. New York: Praeger Publishers, 1976.

Altheide, David L., and Robert P. Snow. *Media Logic*. Beverly Hills, Calif.: Sage Publications, 1979.

Atwell, Robert H., Bruce Grimes, and Donna A. Lopiano. *The Money Game: Financing Collegiate Athletics*. Washington, D.C.: American Council on Education, 1980.

Baker, William J. *Sports in the Western World*. Totowa, N.J.: Littlefield, 1982.

Balbus, Isaac. "Politics as Sports: The Ascendancy of the  Sports Metaphore." *Monthly Review* 6, no. 10 (March 1978):

Ball, D., and John Loy, eds. *Sport and Social Orders*. Reading, Mass.: Addison-Wesley, 1975.

Beerman and Wakefield.

Beisser, Arnold. *Madness in Sports: Psychological Observations on Sports*. New York: Appleton-Century-Crofts, 1967.

Bell, Daniel. *The Coming of Post-Industrial Society*. New York: Basic Books, Inc., 1973.

Betts, John. *America's Sporting Heritage*. Reading, Mass.: Addison-Wesley, 1974.

Boorstin, Daniel J. *The Image*. New York: Athenaeum, 1977.

*Boston Globe,* 4 July 1983.

Boyle, Robert. *Sport: Mirror of American Life*. Boston: Little, Brown, 1963.

Bradley, Bill. *Life on the Run*. New York: Bantam Books, 1977.

Cantor, Muriel G. *Prime Time Television*. Beverly Hills, Calif.: Sage Publications, 1980.

Cater, Douglass, and Richard Adler. *Television as a Social Force: New Approaches to TV Criticism*. New York: Praeger Publishers, 1975.

*Chronicle of Higher Education,* 26 Jan. 1983.

*Chronicle of Higher Education,* 6 July 1983.

*Chronicle of Higher Education,* 26 Oct. 1983.

Chu, Donald. *Dimensions of Sports Studies*. New York: Rowman and Littlefield, 1982.

Cole, Lewis. *A Loose Game: The Sport and Business of Basketball*. Indianapolis, Ind.: Bobbs-Merrill, 1978.

Cosell, Howard. *Cosell*. New York: Pocket Books, 1973.

Cozins, Frederick, and Florence Scovil Stumph. *Sports in American Life.* Chicago: University of Chicago Press, 1953.

Dahl, Robert A. *Dilemmas of Pluralist Democracy.* New Haven: Yale University Press, 1982.

Dahrendorf, Ralf. *Life Chances.* Chicago: University of Chicago Press, 1979.

Davenport, Joanna. "From Crew to Commercialism—The Paradox of Sport in Higher Education." Paper presented at the Conference on Sports and Higher Education, Skidmore College, March 1983.

Davison, W. Phillips, and Frederick T.C. Uyu, eds. *Mass Communication Research: Major Issues and Future Directions.* New York: Praeger Publishers, 1974.

DeFord, Frank. *Big Bill Tilden: The Triumphs and Tragedy.* New York: Simon & Schuster, 1976.

Denlinger, Kenneth Loy, and Leonard Shapiro. *Athletes for Sale.* New York: Thomas Y. Crowell, 1975.

Dennis, Everette E. *The Media Society.* Dubuque, Iowa: William C. Brown Co., 1978.

Dulles, Foster Rhea. *America Learns to Play.* New York: Appleton-Century-Crofts, 1965.

Duncan, Hugh. *Communication and Social Order.* New York: Oxford University Press, 1970.

Durso, Joseph. *The Sports Factory: An Investigation into College Sports.* New York: Quadrangle, 1975.

Edwards, Harry. *The Revolt of the Black Athlete.* New York: The Free Press, 1969.
———. *The Sociology of Sport.* Homewood, Ill.: The Dorsey Press, 1973.

Eitzen, D.S., and G. Sage. *Sociology of American Sport.* Dubuque, Iowa: William C. Brown Co., 1978.

Falla, Jack. *NCAA: The Voice of College Sports.* Shawnee Mission, Kans.: National Collegiate Athletic Association, 1981.

Flood, Curt, with Richard Carter. *The Way It Is.* New York: Pocket Books, 1972.

Freeman, W. "College Athletics in the Twenties: The Golden Age or 'Fool's Gold.' " Paper presented at History Symposiums of the National Association for Sport and Physical Education, Seattle, Wash., April 1977.

Gallico, Paul. *Farewell to Sport.* Freeport, N.Y.: Books for Libraries Press, 1970.

Gans, Herbert J. *Popular Culture and High Culture.* New York: Basic Books, 1974.

Gardner, David P. Cited in *Chronicle of Higher Education,* 13 October 1982.

Geiger, Louis G. *University of the Northern Plains: A History of the University of North Dakota, 1883–1958.*

Grunneau, Richard. *Class, Sports, and Social Development.* Amherst, Mass.: University of Massachusetts Press, 1983.

Gulick, Luther. *A Philosophy of Play.* New York: Charles Scribner's Sons, 1920.

Guttman, Allen. *From Ritual to Record: The Nature of Modern Sports.* New York: Columbia University Press, 1978.

Halberstam, David. *The Breaks of the Game.* New York: Ballantine Books, 1981.

Hart, M. Marie. *Sport in the Socio-Cultural Process.* Dubuque, Iowa: William C. Brown Co., 1972.

Hirsh, Fred. *Social Limits to Growth.* Cambridge: Harvard University Press, 1976.

Hoch, Paul. *Rip Off the Big Game: The Exploitation of Sports by the Power Elite.* New York: Doubleday, 1972.

Huizinga, Johan. *Homo Ludens: A Study of the Play Element in Culture.* Boston: Beacon Press, 1955.

Ibrahim, Hilm. *Sport and Society.* Los Alamitos, Calif.: Hwong Publishing Company, 1976.

Jacobs, Norman, ed. *Culture for the Millions? Mass Media in Modern Society.* Winston, N.J.: D. Van Nostrand Company, 1959.

Jencks, Christopher, and David Riesman. *The Academic Revolution.* Chicago: University of Chicago Press, 1968.

Keller, George. *Academic Strategy.* Baltimore, Md.: Johns Hopkins University Press, 1983.

Kerr, Clark. *The Uses of the University.* Cambridge, Mass.: Harvard University Press, 1982.

Kindred, Dave. *Basketball: The Dream Game in Kentucky.* Louisville, Ky.: Data Courier, Inc., 1976.

Kottak, Conrad Phillip, ed. *Researching American Culture.* Ann Arbor, Mich.: University of Michigan Press, 1982.

Kowet, Don. *The Rich Who Own Sports.* New York: Random House, 1977.

Kramer, Jerry. *Lombardi: Winning Is the Only Thing.* New York: Pocket Books, 1970.

Lasch, Christopher. *The Culture of Narcissism.* New York: Norton-Simon, 1979.

Lewis, Guy L. "Theodore Roosevelt's Role in the 1905 Football Controversy." *Research Quarterly* 40 (December 1969).

Lindblom, Charles E. *Politics in Markets.* New York: Basic Books, 1977.

Lipsky, Richard. *How We Play the Game.* Boston: Beacon Press, 1981.

Lipsyte, Robert. *Sportsworld: An American Dreamland.* New York: Quadrangle, 1976.

Loy, John, and Gerald Kenyon, eds. *Sport, Culture, and Society.* New York: Macmillan, 1969.

Mandell, Richard. *The Nazi Olympics.* New York: Macmillan, 1971.

Meggyesy, Dave. *Out of Their League.* Berkeley, Calif.: Ramparts Press, 1970.

Michener, James. *Sports in America.* New York: Random House, 1976.

*The Miller Lite Report.* Milwaukee, Wis.: 1983.

Morison, Samuel Eliot. *Harvard College in the Seventeenth Century.* Cambridge: Harvard University Press, 1936.

National Collegiate Athletic Association. *1983 Convention Proceedings.* San Diego, Calif.: NCAA, 1983.

Nelson, David. "Governance of Intercollegiate Athletics—Who Is Running the Asylum?" Paper presented to the Conference on Sports and Higher Education, Skidmore College, March 1983.

*New York Times,* 14 July 1983, sec. B, p. 14.

Noll, Roger, ed. *Government and the Sports Business.* Washington, D.C.: The Brookings Institution, 1974.

Novak, Michael. *The Joy of Sports.* New York: Basic Books, 1976.

Offen, Neil. *The Black Athlete: A Shameful Story.* New York: Time-Life Books, 1969.

———. *God Save the Players.* Chicago: Playboy Press, 1974.

Olsen, Jack. *The Black Athlete.* New York: Time-Life Books, 1968.

Paul, William Henry. *The Gray-Flannel Pigskins: Movers and Shakers of Pro Football.* Philadelphia: Lippincott, 1974.

Perry, Ralph Barton. *Puritanism and Democracy.* New York: Vanguard, 1944.

Peterson, Robert. *Only the Ball Was White.* Englewood Cliffs, N.J.: Prentice-Hall, 1970.

Plimpton, George. *Mad Ducks and Bears.* New York: Random House, 1973.

———. *Paper Lion.* New York: Pocket Books, 1967.

Raiborn, Mitchell. *Revenues and Expenses of Intercollegiate Athletic Programs.* Shawnee Mission, Kans.: National Collegiate Athletic Association, 1978 and 1982.

Raspberry, William. "A Pay Plan for College Athletes." *Pittsburgh Press,* 17 March 1983, sec. B, p. 2.

Rooney, John L., Jr., *A Geography of American Sport: From Cabin Creek to Anaheim.* Reading, Mass.: Addison-Wesley, 1974.

———. "Intercollegiate Athletic Recruiting: A Geographical Analysis of Its Origin, Diffusion and Potential Demise." *Phi Kappa Phi Journal* (Winter 1982):

———. *The Recruiting Game.* Lincoln, Neb.: University of Nebraska Press, 1980.

Rudolph, Frederick. *The American College and University: A History.* New York: Vintage Books, 1962.

Sage, George, ed. *Sport and American Society.* Reading, Mass.: Addison-Wesley, 1970.

Sagendorph, Kent. *Michigan: The Story of the University.* Ann Arbor, Mich.: University of Michigan Press,

Savage, Howard J. *American College Athletics.* New York: The Carnegie Foundation for the Advancement of Teaching, 1929.

Scattsneider, E.E. *The Semi-Sovereign People.* New York: Holt, 1960.

Schiller, Herbert I. *The Mind Managers.* Boston: Beacon Press, 1973.

Scott, Jack. *The Athletic Revolution.* New York: The Free Press, 1971.

Shaw, Gary. *Meat on the Hoof.* New York: St. Martin's Press, 1973.

Shils, Edward. *Center and Periphery: Essays in Macro-Sociology.* Chicago: University of Chicago Press, 1975.

Singletary, Otis A. "Getting Presidents More Involved in College Sports; Developing the Proper Role." *New York Times,* 8 January 1984, sec. S, p. 2.

Sklar, Robert. *Prime-Time America: Life On and Behind the Television Screen.* New York: Oxford University Press, 1980.

Sojka, Gregory S. "The Evolution of the Student-Athlete in America: From Divinity to the Divine." Paper presented at the Conference on Sports and Higher Education, Skidmore College, March 1982.

*Sporting News,* 23 May 1983.

*Sporting News,* 4 July 1983.

*Sports Illustrated,* 31 Aug. 1981.

*Sports Illustrated,* 16 Nov. 1981.

*Sports Illustrated,* 30 Nov. 1981.

*Sports Illustrated,* 28 Sept. 1982.

Stebbins, Robert A. *Amateurs.* Beverly Hills, Calif.: Sage Publications, 1979.

Stone, *The Hidden Election.*

Talamini, John, and Charles Page, eds. *Sport and Society: An Anthology.* Boston: Little, Brown, 1973.

Tenney, Sanborn Gove. "Athletics at Williams." *Outing* 17 (1890).

Thurow, Lester C. *The Zero-Sum Society.* New York: Basic Books, 1980.

Touraine, Alain. *The Academic System in American Society.* New York: McGraw-Hill Book Company, 1974.

Tutko, Thomas, and William Burns. *Winning Is Everything, and Other American Myths.* New York: Macmillan, 1976.

Vance, N. Scott. "Making It to a Football Bowl Takes More Than a Good Record." *Chronicle of Higher Education* 25, no. 14.

Visser, Lesley. "Atlantic Coast or Gold Coast?" *Boston Globe,* date?

———. "College Boosters: Out of Control?" *Boston Globe,* 3 July 1983.

———. "The Sales Pitch Is Packing Them In." *Boston Globe,* 5 July 1983.

*Wall Street Journal,* 16 October 1980.

*Washington Post,* 11 July 1983.

Wayand, Alexander M. *The Sage of American Football Development.* New York: Macmillan, 1955.

Weiss, Paul. *Sport: A Philosophic Inquiry.* Carbondale, Ill.: Southern Illinois University Press, 1969.

Welborn, David W. *Governance of Federal Regulatory Agencies.* Knoxville, Tenn.: University of Tennessee Press, 1977.

White, Gordon S., Jr. "NCAA Overseer Proposed." *New York Times,* 16 December 1983, sec. B. p. 7.

Wood, Peter H. "Television As a Dream." In *Television As a Cultural Force,* edited by Richard Adler and Douglass Cater. New York: Praeger Publishers, 1976.

Yankelovich, Daniel. *New Rules: Searching for Self-Fulfillment in a World Turned Upside Down.* Toronto: Bantam Books, 1981.

# Index

# About the Authors

**Nand Hart-Nibbrig** is an associate professor of public administration and adjunct professor of political science at West Virginia University. Prior to coming to West Virginia University, he taught courses in political science, public administration, and public affairs at Arizona State University, the Navajo Nation, the University of Southern California, the University of Washington, California State University at San Jose, and Long Beach City College. He received his B.A. and M.A. in political science from the University of California at Los Angeles (UCLA) and his Ph.D. in political science from the University of California, Berkeley. He has published in the areas of state and local government, intergovernmental relations, public policy, school desegregation policy, and higher education policy.

Mr. Hart-Nibbrig is active in matters which affect higher education generally and West Virginia University specifically. In this regard he has served on the President's Academic Planning Committee, the Black Community Concerns Committee, the Martin R. Delany Committee for Visiting Scholars (serving as its first chairman), the Financial Exigency Committee; the Housing Committee and Information Liaison Council for the College of Arts and Sciences, and the search committee for the vice president for academic affairs/provost.

**Clement Cottingham** is an associate professor of political science at Rutgers University, Newark. He also has taught political science at the University of California, Swarthmore College, the University of Pennsylvania, and Vanderbilt University. He has previously written articles and coedited books on ethnic politics, urban poverty, and comparative politics in less developed countries. Presently, he is at work on a study of political crises and modernization in postcolonial Africa.

## DATE DUE

| | | |
|---|---|---|
| OCT 15 1986 | JAN 02 1997 | |
| JAN 1987 | OCT 2 0 1997 | |
| NOV 1987 | NOV 2 6 1997 | |
| FEB 1 1988 | | |
| APR 4 1988 | FEB 0 1 1999 | |
| MAY 23 1988 | | |
| | MAY 1 6 1999 | |
| | JUL 3 1 1999 | |
| APR 3 1989 | | |
| MAY 2 | NOV 28 1999 | |
| NOV 2 0 1989 | SEP 0 5 2000 | |
| MAY 28 1990 | SEP 0 1 2001 | |
| DEC 1 7 1990 | | |
| | FEB 0 1 2002 | |
| OCT 2 8 1991 | | |
| AUG 1 1 1994 | | |
| NOV 1 7 1994 | | |
| APR 2 7 1995 | | |
| MAY 2 2 1996 | | |
| SEP 0 1 1996 | | |